The CILIP Guidelines for Secondary School Libraries

The CILIP Guidelines for Secondary School Libraries

Edited by
Lynn Barrett and **Jonathan Douglas**
for the School Libraries Group of CILIP

Working Group
Eileen Armstrong, Lynn Barrett, Jonathan Douglas, Liz Dubber, Steve Hird, Sue Jones, Annette Lear, Gill Purbrick, Anne-Marie Tarter, Glenys Willars

© CILIP: the Chartered Institute of Library and Information Professionals, 1998, 2004

Published by
Facet Publishing
7 Ridgmount Street
London WC1E 7AE

Facet Publishing (formerly Library Association Publishing) is wholly owned by CILIP: the Chartered Institute of Library and Information Professionals.

Except as otherwise permitted under the Copyright, Designs and Patents Act 1988 this publication may only be reproduced, stored or transmitted in any form or by any means, with the prior permission of the publisher, or, in the case of reprographic reproduction, in accordance with the terms of a licence issued by The Copyright Licensing Agency. Enquiries concerning reproduction outside those terms should be sent to Facet Publishing, 7 Ridgmount Street, London WC1E 7AE.

First published under the title *Library Association Guidelines for Secondary School Libraries* in 1998
This second edition 2004

British Library Cataloguing in Publication Data
A catalogue record for this book is available from the British Library.

ISBN 1-85604-481-5

Typeset from editors' disks by Facet Publishing Production in 10.5/14pt Nimbus Roman and Nimbus Sans.
Printed and made in Great Britain by MPG Books Ltd, Bodmin, Cornwall.

Contents

Foreword *Rt Hon. Charles Clarke MP* **vii**

Ofsted on libraries and learning   ix

Key recommendations   xi

Introduction   xiii

Glossary   xvi

1   **The school library and learning: CILIP's vision   1**

2   **School library policy and development planning   7**

3   **The management of the school library   11**

4   **Facilities management   23**

5   **Management of learning resources   31**

6   **Information literacy   37**

7   **Reader development   47**

8   **Marketing, promotion and advocacy   55**

9   **Evaluation   67**

10   **Partnerships   77**

Bibliography and further reading   85

Appendix 1
Library policy template   91

Appendix 2
Development plan template   93

Appendix 3
Sample job description for a secondary school librarian   94

Appendix 4
Sample template for budget planning   96

Appendix 5
Risk assessment form   97

Appendix 6
E-learning and virtual learning environments   98

Appendix 7
Facilities management checklist   101

Appendix 8
Research grid   104

Appendix 9
Mind mapping   105

Index   109

Foreword

I am pleased to be able to officially endorse these *Guidelines* which, I am sure, will provide librarians and school leadership teams with the focus and direction needed to develop the library's central function within their schools.

The school library is the heart of a school, which itself has learning at its core, and good libraries can empower the learner. The resources in a library can allow our imaginations to run free, introduce us to new experiences and promote access to knowledge and enjoyment. Further, it is important for students to become independent users of information, but for this to occur it is vital that they are given the skills to learn how to find this information, how to select what is relevant, and how to use it in the best way for their own particular needs and take responsibility for their own learning.

School libraries can also help teachers to use a broader range of teaching strategies. Project work, individual study, group research, reading and the teaching of ICT, amongst other things, can all take place in the school library. In providing this flexible place for learning, teachers themselves are encouraged to widen and enrich their own teaching. By supporting and giving access to a broad range of information sources the school library can motivate students and stimulate learning by providing the means to freely pursue subjects that fully engage them.

To do these things the librarian must work collaboratively with teaching colleagues and with management to raise standards of learning and teaching throughout the school community by increasing the levels of excellence in school library provision. This document will provide valuable guidance in this endeavour and I wish you well.

Rt Hon. Charles Clarke MP
Secretary of State for Education and Skills

Foreword

Ofsted on libraries and learning

Our inspection evidence consistently shows that a good, well-managed library or learning resource centre in a school enriches the learning experience of pupils and contributes much to their enthusiasm for reading. Also, where pupils read more widely the quality of their writing and range of their vocabulary are almost always better than in schools where reading is not fostered.

Peter Daw
Specialist Adviser with responsibility for libraries, Ofsted

Key recommendations

CILIP recommends that:

1 The school see the contribution of the school library and the librarian as key priorities in all plans for whole-school improvement.

2 The school have a library policy and a development plan that reflect the needs of the school, its students and teachers.

3 The school recognize the essential management role of the librarian and seek to appoint a full-time chartered librarian with administrative support.

4 The physical environment of the school library should support its role as a whole-school learning resource at the heart of the school community.

5 The school support the vital role that quality resources play in stimulating learning with recommended levels of investment (providing 13 items per student) and that it seek to maximize the impact of this investment by managing resources centrally.

6 The school commit itself to the development of information-literate students who are able to become independent, lifelong learners, and sees the librarian taking a lead role in this development.

7 The school librarian play a lead role in developing a whole-school reading culture, promoting literacy and reading for pleasure.

8 The school library be proactively marketed in response to evidence-based analysis of the needs of all potential users.

9 The school library evaluate its performance regularly through a programme of self-evaluation agreed with the school's senior management.

10 The school librarian work in partnership with key internal and external partners to improve the quality of the school library.

Introduction

These *Guidelines* are the recommendations of CILIP: the Chartered Institute of Library and Information Professionals for the effective management of secondary school libraries. They are primarily directed to those who manage school libraries – as practical guidance and material for advocacy. They are also addressed to headteachers, governors and all who are involved in the strategic management of education and who require an understanding of what is required.

The Library Association's *Guidelines for Secondary School Libraries*[1] have been highly influential in guiding the development of secondary school libraries. They provided a powerful vision for advocacy and offered a practical framework for school library management. This document rediscovers that framework in the context of a rapidly changing education and library landscape and is a major step forward in CILIP's vision of library provision in secondary schools.

Following consultation with a wide range of stakeholders, a working group was established by CILIP's School Libraries Group (SLG) comprising:

Eileen Armstrong Librarian, Cramlington Community High School

Lynn Barrett Information Services Manager, Dixons Technology College, Bradford

Jonathan Douglas Head of Learning and Access, Museums, Libraries and Archives Council (Jonathan was Youth and School Libraries Adviser, CILIP, when editing these *Guidelines*)

Liz Dubber Assistant Head of Libraries and Information, Gloucestershire

Steve Hird Manager, Rotherham Schools Library Service

Sue Jones Manager, Hertfordshire Schools Library Service (representing ASCEL)

Annette Lear Librarian, Oakham School

Gill Purbrick SLG Councillor, CILIP, and Chair, School Libraries Group

Anne-Marie Tarter Librarian, Ripon Grammar School

Glenys Willars Learning and Information Development Manager, Leicestershire Library Services.

This update of the 1998 *Guidelines* was prompted by new thinking about information literacy, reader development and information communication technologies. The working group also considered important new policy themes:

- the importance of young people's participation in library development, based on CILIP's adoption of *Start with the Child*,[2] which stresses the importance of young people's contribution to service definition and design
- the development of school libraries based on rigorous investigation of needs and self-evaluation
- inclusion.

At the heart of these *Guidelines* are ten recommendations (see page xi) that are the foundations of excellent school library provision. CILIP hopes that these recommendations will be accepted and implemented in every secondary school. Being aware that its vision for school library provision depends on partnerships with a wide range of stakeholders, CILIP also commends these *Guidelines* to the attention of education managers, policy makers and government.

The working group has made use of many experts in writing these *Guidelines*. Special thanks go to Liz Dubber, Assistant Head of Libraries and Information, Gloucestershire, for her assistance with the final editing. Contributions from the following people have also been appreciated:

Marie Costigan and **Dan Philips** at the Department for Education and Skills
Peter Daw Specialist Adviser with responsibility for libraries, Oftsted
Professor Judith Elkin Vice Principal, University College Worcester
Kathy Lemaire and the **School Library Association**
Sue Horner QCA
Neil McClelland Director, National Literacy Trust
Bob Wilkes Manager, Education Bradford Library Service
The School Libraries Group of the Education Publishers' Council.

References

1 Tilke, A. (ed.), *Library Association Guidelines for Secondary School Libraries*, Library Association Publishing, 1998.

2 *Start with the Child: the needs and motivations of young people, a report commissioned by Resource and the Chartered Institute of Library and Information Professionals*, CILIP, 2002, www.resource.gov.uk/documents/re179rep.pdf.

Note

Many school libraries are now known as learning resource centres, LRCs or open learning centres. Similarly, the school librarian may be called the learning resource centre manager. In this document the terms 'school library' and 'school librarian' are used to refer to all of the above.

Glossary

AASL	American Association of School Librarians
ALA	American Library Association
ASLA	Australian School Library Association
AIDA	Marketing mnemonic standing for *A*wareness, *I*nterest, *D*esire, *A*ction
CILIP	The Chartered Institute of Library and Information Professionals
Connexions	Service that provides a single point of access for all 13–19 year-olds to help them prepare for the transition to work and adult life
CPD	continuing professional development
DfES	Department for Education and Skills
ECDL	European Computer Driving Licence
IASL	International Association of School Librarianship
ICT	information and communication technology
IFLA	International Federation of Library Associations
INSET	in-service education and training
MLE	managed learning environment
OECD	Organization for Economic Co-operation and Development
Ofsted	Office for Standards in Education
PTA	parent teacher association
SLA	School Library Association
SLG	School Libraries Group
SLS	schools library service
UNESCO	United Nations Educational, Scientific and Cultural Organization
VLE	virtual learning environment
WAN	wide area network

1

The school library and learning: CILIP's vision

CILIP recommends that the school see the contribution of the school library and the librarian as key priorities in all plans for whole-school improvement.

The school library provides learning services, books and resources that enable all members of the school community to become critical thinkers and effective users of information in all formats and media, with links to the wider library and information network, according to the principles in the UNESCO Public Library Manifesto.
The School Library Manifesto[1]

Learning is a process of active engagement with experience. It is what people do when they want to make sense of the world. It may involve an increase in skills, knowledge, understanding, values and the capacity to reflect. Effective learning leads to change, development and a desire to learn more.
Definition of learning, Campaign for Learning[2]

The school library empowers learning: it gives access to real and virtual environments where learners can discover resources that inspire and develop them. These learners may be students, teachers, their families or the wider community. Through using the library as a learning resource centre they all share in the knowledge, information and works of the creative imagination to which it provides access.

School libraries are more vibrant today than ever before. Learning resources are more varied and attractive. Exciting new technologies offer fresh ways of understanding the world. Access to libraries is no longer defined by physical access. New and innovative ways of promoting literature and encouraging readers underpin all these developments.

At the same time there is evidence of an increasing focus by government departments on school library provision. This is an acknowledgement of the key role libraries have to play in delivering national policies, particularly in increasing literacy and establishing lifelong learning.[3]

In the knowledge society, the skills and opportunities to access, assess and use information represent a basic learning entitlement. The internet will not replace the school library; rather, it is a powerful reason for schools to enhance the role of the library as the hub of the school's information strategy.

This chapter explores how the school librarian and the school library inspire learning. CILIP believes that school libraries have a key role to play in realizing the vision for education that the Government has outlined in key policy documents such as *A New Specialist System: transforming secondary education*.[4] It is important that headteachers, governors and other key decision-makers share this vision. Low expectations of what the school library can deliver will undermine the library's contribution. These guidelines aim to raise expectations and support schools with a framework for realizing them.

How the school library supports learning

The school librarian is the champion of the learner. Therefore, the focus of all library services and activities is the learner. The school librarian creates a variety of interactions with teachers and students in order to stimulate real learning. Some of these are obvious (teaching information handling skills, delivering in-service education and training (INSET) for teachers, offering reading groups and providing high quality teaching and learning resources) and some are hidden (motivating and advising individual students' reading choices and supporting drop-in provision). However, all are vital to creating a whole-school environment where information is valued and used effectively and where reading is fostered, treasured and enjoyed.

New technologies present new opportunities for learning. Time, space and cultural barriers disappear as electronic access and virtual communities emerge. The library must be the gateway to these virtual environments of learning. It must be a resource centre rich in all media, where access is supported and facilitated by an information expert.

The school librarian as mediator

The variety of roles required of the school librarian to bring CILIP's vision for school libraries to life can be described as follows.

The librarian facilitates learning through:

- helping teachers and students to access relevant information
- developing their skills to use this information independently.

The librarian and the library motivate learning by:

- stimulating individual curiosities that lie at the heart of the desire to learn
- providing access to resources at a variety of levels
- meeting the unique needs of individual learners and inspiring their own interests.

The library validates and supports individual learners' interests outside the curriculum through:

- relating to students' own interests with immediately relevant materials
- harnessing their self-motivated learning, thus creating learners for life.

The librarian teaches through:

- collaborating with colleagues to enrich students' experiences with information
- developing an information-literacy curriculum in partnership with teaching colleagues that is delivered through the curriculum
- delivering information literacy INSET sessions to staff.

Another crucial way in which the school library supports the learner is by stimulating leisure reading. Increasingly, research is demonstrating the correlation between reading for pleasure and skill acquisition.[5] The school librarian is uniquely equipped to promote reading within the school. As a book and reading expert the librarian can deploy knowledge and instil enthusiasm. Operating outside of any particular department, the librarian is ideally placed to develop strategies aimed at creating a whole-school reading community and helping the emotional development of individual students.

The library is a unique space within the school. It is not a classroom or a common room. It is the home of independent study and self-directed learning, as well as individual and collaborative research. It is truly an extension of the classroom. It is also unique in that it offers a neutral space to students of all abilities and personalities without judgement. It is the place where the student with learning difficulties may be found working comfortably next to the Oxbridge-bound student.

Finally, the school library shares in the overall mission of the school. The library is a central element of a whole-school approach to learning and has a vital role to play in raising achievement. It is important that all plans for improving the school in any sphere take account of the potential role of the school library.

The school library and the wider learning community

Loaning items from the school library means that its resources enter the homes of students and teachers. In this and a host of other ways (such as longer opening hours, out-of-hours learning activities, community-access entitlements, virtual/dialup access) the school library spreads it influence beyond the school building into the leisure times and family lives of students. But beyond these informal links with the wider community, school libraries need to sit at the heart of a network of learning partnerships (see Chapter 10).

Partnerships between the school library and other institutions enhance the partnerships that the school requires to engage effectively with the community. School libraries have an important part to play in developing the extended role of secondary schools. Partnerships that support the vocational education of students in colleges, local workplaces and institutions of higher education must include co-ordination of learning resource management. Community learning-resource partnerships are already emerging in some places with school librarians taking a lead role.

A key partnership for the secondary school library will be with the schools library service (SLS), the central library support service provided by the local authority. The services offered by SLSs have become increasingly diverse, but they all aim to support library provision in schools and raise student achievement. The SLS is a key contact, supporting the dissemination of best school library practice, enabling the economic resourcing of school libraries and providing advice, guidance and training for school librarians, teaching staff and senior management.

Another important partnership is with local primary schools. The library environment will be one of the few constants between primary and secondary schools and should play an important role in the transition between the two. It is essential that primary and secondary schools have a consistent approach to acquiring information skills and a mutually supportive approach to reader development.

The school library's primary partner will always be the learner. CILIP believes that the school library must treat students as active partners – moving from engaging them in consultation on the development of services and resources, to encouraging them to participate fully not just in operational activities but in the whole range of library management activities.[6] This way the library will truly be relevant to all learners in the school and effectively become the champion of the learner.

Notes and references

1 IFLA/UNESCO, *The School Library Manifesto*, IFLA, 2000, www.ifla.org/VII/s11/pubs/manifest.htm.
2 Campaign for Learning, www.campaign-for-learning.org.uk.
3 Reflected in England by the creation of the DfES School Libraries Working Group in 2001.
4 DfES, *A New Specialist System: transforming secondary education*, 2003.
5 OECD, *Reading for Change: performance and engagement across countries*, 2002, www.pisa.oecd.org/Docs/Download/ReadingExeSummary.pdf.
6 National Youth Agency, *Hear by Right*, National Youth Agency, 2003, www.4youthinc.co.uk/hear.htm.

2

School library policy and development planning

CILIP recommends that the school have a library policy and a development plan that reflect the needs of the school, its students and its teachers.

There are two main vehicles for articulating and achieving the vision for the school library. These are the **library policy** and the **development plan**.

The library needs to state explicitly how it will realize the vision of its role as explored in Chapter 1. This is expressed by developing the library's aims and objectives in a policy document. The development plan document sets out how these aims and objectives will be achieved by setting targets, establishing time frames and costings and detailing measurable outcomes. Although the templates in the Appendices 1 and 2 may be used as a guide, each library should adopt the policy and development plan styles already in use by the school.

The school library policy

The policy document defines how the library will help deliver the aims and mission of the school. It reflects the ethos, aspirations and changing priorities of the whole school community. At the same time, it provides a practical framework for managing the school library and realizing its full potential.

It is essential that the process of developing the policy is shared as widely as possible. Many school library policies are successfully developed through forming a working group that can provide a focus for wider stakeholder engagement. It is essential that the school's teaching staff is fully aware and supportive of the school library policy. It is also important to invite external partners, such as the schools library service, literacy advisers and other local education librarians to participate in developing a policy. They will bring experience to the process and will ensure it is part of the strategy for learning resource provision in the wider community.

While each school library policy is a unique document, each will define the role of the school library in relation to:

- the curriculum and key education strategies
- learning and teaching methods within the school
- national standards and recommendations
- students' learning and developmental/pastoral needs
- teachers' learning and teaching needs
- raising achievement
- inspiring readers
- promoting information literacy.

Therefore a school library policy will generally include:

- aims and objectives of the school library
- the management structure and systems of the school library
- user and non-user involvement in the library's management
- resource management guidelines
- how the library contributes to information skill development across the curriculum
- how the library promotes reading across the school
- how the library caters for individual learning needs to ensure equal access for all
- a commitment to key external relations – especially with the schools library service
- how the school library is promoted
- how the school library is monitored and evaluated
- how and when the school library policy is to be revised.

The school library policy is not a static document. It should be reviewed annually at a formal meeting of the senior management team (SMT), the library committee or the governing body, as deemed appropriate. The purpose of such a review is to update the policy to reflect changes and development in the library and respond to priorities in the school community as a whole.

Chapter 2 School library policy and development planning

The school library development plan

The development plan sets out to achieve the vision for the library that lies at the heart of the school library policy. The development plan is essentially an action plan which (like the library policy) must be built on consultation and open communication with all stakeholders. It is key that the development plan is based on the agenda of the whole school and is not just a reflection of library priorities. It should make explicit references to how the library will be delivering the main goals of the organization, such as raising literacy levels, or maximizing the learning opportunities offered by ICT. It should build on the findings of inspection or self-evaluation exercises.

Library development plans will usually be medium term, covering three to five years. They need to coincide with the school's planning cycle.

The development planning process will involve:

1 consultation with senior management about key development priorities for the whole school
2 consultation with users and non-users about library development priorities
3 definition of goals, objectives and desired outcomes linked to priorities and the identification of success criteria
4 assessment of the current position of the library, making reference to self-evaluation undertaken, audit of inputs against national guidance and an honest appraisal of current activities
5 identification of development actions to deliver defined outcomes and analysis of any professional development needs of school library staff or partners
6 analysis of the financial implications of development
7 indication of the timeframe within which the objectives will be achieved
8 development of key partnerships, internal and external to the school
9 implementation and monitoring (including performance measures to be used)
10 evaluation and communication of impact of development to staff and students (including appropriate performance indicators to demonstrate progress against the objectives).

Stakeholder involvement in policy and plan development

The school librarian needs to deploy a number of strategies to ensure that library policy and development plans accurately reflect the needs of stakeholders and are supported by the whole school community and the school's senior management.

The library committee

Committees should be led by the school librarian and may be established to support the development of the library either on a long-term basis or with a fixed-term project focus. Either way it is necessary that they have the full support of senior management and a membership that reflects the interests of the whole school community, with representatives from:

- senior management
- the governing body
- senior teachers or departmental representatives
- users and non-users – both staff and students.

The library committee can have an important role in planning, drawing up development plans and winning support for library policy. It demonstrates that the school library is owned as a whole-school resource and is at the heart of learning and teaching within the school.

User consultation

In order to meet user needs effectively, it is necessary to consult frequently with users and non-users about what they want from the school library. Focus groups, interactive exhibitions and displays, consultations with teachers and students, qualitative as well as quantitative information, user and non-user surveys, and informal conversations, all provide useful evidence to inform development planning. It is important that the school library publicizes action prompted by the findings of consultation. This increases staff and students' ownership of the library and encourages them to participate in future consultation. Qualitative and quantitative evidence-gathering and methods of consultation are dealt with more fully in Chapter 9.

Policy and development plan endorsement

In order to win recognition and support for the school library it is important that the policy and the development plan are communicated to the senior management team and also to governors. Student councils and student forums also need to know about and support plans for library development and can be informed through meetings, Powerpoint presentations, displays, written reports, school newspapers and bulletins, etc. Advocates, such as library-link governors, can also help promote awareness of the results of consultations, evaluations and plans for development.

3

The management of the school library

CILIP recommends that the school recognize the essential management role of the librarian and seek to appoint a full-time chartered librarian with administrative support.

The management of the school library will determine the impact the library has on achievement. Research has shown that where the school's senior management actively supports and endorses the librarian's management of the school library, then the library is more effective in supporting key educational initiatives.[1] Research has also demonstrated that where a skilled librarian is empowered by management to collaborate effectively with teaching departments then the library's impact on learning is optimized.[2] However, it has also been shown that a major factor in realizing the impact of the library on the whole school is the individual school librarian. The learning librarian is a reflective practitioner: one who keeps up to date, looks for opportunities for professional development, is a member of professional organizations, seeks to understand teaching and learning and knows the curriculum. Assuming that a learning librarian is in post, this chapter lays out the management responsibilities of the school librarian and explores how the role fits into the whole educational structure.

The school librarian within the school management structure

The management of the library must reflect and support school policies (e.g.

behaviour codes, inclusion, promotional activities, etc.). To achieve this, librarians must be integrated into the school's management structure at a high enough level to have impact. They must be able to make decisions about appropriate support for curriculum initiatives and development. To enable this to happen, **CILIP recommends that the librarian**:

- **be line managed by the senior management team member with responsibility for curriculum development, and have direct access to the strategic management of the school, so that the library can play a full role in school development**

- **have head of department status so that the librarian can listen to, understand and meet the needs of all departments within the school and play a full and proactive part in school management**

- **collaborate with all departments in the planning and the delivery of curriculum-based information skills and literacy programmes**

- **be included in all staff appraisals and training and participate in the delivery of relevant staff INSETs.**

The school librarian should not be associated with any one particular teaching department, but needs to work effectively across the curriculum.

A specimen job description for a chartered school librarian appears in Appendix 3. CILIP publishes a full salary guide for school libraries which is available on the CILIP website (www.lisjobnet.org.uk/jobseek/school.pdf) or in hard copy on application.

The management responsibilities of the librarian fall into a number of different categories, some of which are detailed in this chapter, and some in other parts of these *Guidelines*, as indicated:

- financial planning and budget management
- human resources and CPD
- behaviour management
- management of ICT
- development planning (see Chapter 2)
- facilities management (see Chapter 4)
- resources management (see Chapter 5)
- marketing, promotion and advocacy (see Chapter 8)
- evaluation (see Chapter 9)
- partnership management (see Chapter 10).

Financial planning and budget management

Financial planning and budget management are the two processes that govern all library funding. A sample budget can be found in Appendix 4.

Financial planning

Sound financial planning must precede budget management. To be seen as authoritative, it must be based on the following:

- standards and guidelines
- the library's development plan, which is based on the whole-school development plan
- educational initiatives
- historical spend and planning for future developments
- capital projects.

Standards and guidelines

Standards and guidelines are useful tools in identifying the library's current position, which should be reviewed annually. The service should be benchmarked against that which is recommended as well as that which is considered to be best practice. The librarian will be familiar with the latter through professional reading, active partnership with the local schools library service and involvement in professional organizations.

Development plan

The financial requirements of the library's development must be related to whole-school targets and detailed in the library's development plan. The value of a three-year plan is that it can detail expenditure required to fulfil a target in the first year and outline what will be needed to take the action forward in following years. Areas that require a rolling programme of funds should be identified, such as IT hardware replacement and electronic subscriptions.

Educational initiatives

Both national and local initiatives that impact on the library's services and resources are part of the financial planning process. Examples include curriculum changes, literacy programmes, ICT developments and new courses on offer. It is necessary to establish whether software or electronic subscriptions will be accessible across the school network. If so, the argument for central funding is strong, taking the pressure off the library budget. Departmental support should be sought for cross-curricular resources.

Historical spend and future planning

Previous years' expenditures should be analysed and include elements for stock, periodicals, stationery, photocopying and maintenance/support contracts on equipment and software. This will help to build a picture of requirements and form the basis of a new budget request.

Future developments in the school and specific directions for the library need to be taken into account. Known costs or reasonable estimates should be indicated in order to provide senior management with the facts to support sound financial planning. Opportunities to access external sources of funding should be identified.

Capital projects

Capital projects are one-off spends that are not part of the school's annual funding from which a budget is allocated. They might be for new furnishings, computer hardware and/or software (such as a library management system), or even for new resources needed to deliver a specific student learning outcome.

Requests for capital spend should be related to outcomes that are measurable, such as reduced loss resulting from the installation of a security system. A bid should indicate the benefits to users as well as how the benefits will be measured. Where appropriate, it should include quotations for the proposed spend.

Budget management

Once a budget has been allocated, it must be well managed. It is useful to plan how funds will be spent over the 10 months of the academic year. Some institutions require this type of detailed planning, but even if they do not, it is sound management practice to be able to predict when money will be required from each budget section and to be able to account for funds already committed or spent. While periodicals may require a monthly expenditure, it is wise to complete spending for most other resources before the end of the financial year as funds may be curtailed to cover other unexpected costs within the school rather than carried forward into the next financial year. Also, future budgets may be cut as a result.

At any given time the library should be able to provide a breakdown of what has been spent to date. As different schools will require different levels of detail, it may be useful to be able to break this down by department, year groups or resource type or format. Negotiating an allocation from the library's budget for individual departments will not only indicate how funds have been spent across the whole curriculum, but also provide a means of tracking the use of resources to justify increasing or decreasing allocations in future years. It may be useful to instigate a rolling programme for spending across departments to keep resources

Chapter 3 The management of the school library

up to date or to consider cost-sharing with departments for more expensive or electronic resources.

Human resources and CPD

Staffing arrangements in secondary school libraries differ widely throughout the UK, as shown in the *Survey of Secondary School Libraries*.[3] CILIP recommends that a full-time chartered librarian manage the library, supported by library assistants. Where libraries are provided in a school on more than one site, it is important that both sites are staffed full time.

In the case of solo librarians in schools, it is important that the librarian is able to manage his/her time effectively and professionally, enabling adequate time to be spent working with students and teaching colleagues while ensuring adequate breaks in line with current health and safety requirements. A good way to raise senior management's awareness of the amount of time required for housekeeping tasks is to do a time and motion study and show the number of staff-hours required to carry out all functions of the library effectively. This can provide an effective basis for a request for library assistants or administrative support.

School librarians should be part of the school's performance management scheme with:

- an annual review of performance
- an annual review of the post's job description and grading
- targets, at least one of which should focus on student learning and/or attainment and one on professional development
- regular discussions with the line manager during the year
- a focus always on positive development or support where necessary
- access to relevant external training and development opportunities.

In cases where library assistants are present, it is important that they are well managed by the librarian. This means:

- attention to on-the-job training
- ongoing communication
- appraisal following the above model
- inclusion in whole staff INSET training
- access to external training, such as appropriate levels of NVQs.[4]

Student librarians play an important role in the running of many school libraries. They too need to be trained, given responsibility, and appraised. Many are able to complete NVQs at level 2, which gives them not only internal

16 The CILIP Guidelines for Secondary School Libraries

recognition and expertise, but a national qualification as well.

Continuous professional development (CPD)

Rapid development in librarianship, information management, ICT and in the education sector means that it is essential that the school librarian actively engage in CPD. This may encompass a wide variety of activity from temporary placements, participation in training, and professional reading to active networking, committee involvement and higher educational qualifications.

Librarians should ensure that they are part of the school's own INSET and CPD opportunities and contribute to curriculum and pastoral days both benefiting from and, where appropriate, delivering INSET.

Librarians need to manage their own continuous professional development in co-operation with the school's staff development officer. It is useful to maintain a professional development portfolio and to use it as the basis for the annual appraisal. The librarian must have access to external training opportunities and be able to attend appropriate meetings and exhibitions. It is also vital that the librarian has time to network with other local school librarians.

In order to develop professionally, school librarians need to participate actively in professional groups and networks in a setting wider than the school, where they will frequently be the only information professional. CILIP, the CILIP School Libraries Group, membership of local schools library services and the School Library Association provide excellent opportunities for professional participation. Web-based communities and e-lists can also provide invaluable opportunities for librarians to participate in professional discussion. Some of these resources are listed at the end of this chapter.

Behaviour management

In order to manage behaviour effectively, it is necessary to understand the way children learn, the barriers to learning and responses that these provoke, and how to communicate with young people in a variety of contexts. Unlike teachers, librarians are unlikely to receive any formal training in behaviour management through their initial professional qualification, so it is important that opportunities to attend courses and INSET sessions addressing the topic are made available to them.

Many librarians have legitimate concerns about the number of students they have to supervise at peak periods. Advice from the Professional Association of Teachers (PAT) indicates that there are no national guidelines for supervision ratios in libraries. However, clearly the library does need to be included in the school's risk assessment procedures, from which the necessary level of supervision should emerge. A sample risk assessment form appears in Appendix 5.

Chapter 3 The management of the school library **17**

In addition, it is important that all health and safety issues are dealt with effectively and the risk assessment will also highlight any hazards, such as unsafe furniture or flooring, unstable shelves, etc. While there is no legal requirement for the librarians to be first aiders, if they are they will be in a position to help if a child is injured or ill. Alternatively, the librarian will need to know how to call for a first aider. There need to be procedures in place to deal with any medical emergency that may arise in the library.

PAT further advises that, although there is no legislation prescribing adult/student ratios in school libraries, each school should check with its LEA to see if any recommendations have been made. In any event, it is the school's responsibility to organize staff so as to maintain reasonable supervision of children, and the relevant factors will be:

- the children: their age, maturity, etc.; there may be no history of misbehaviour, but on the other hand there may be some/regular breaches of discipline
- the supervisor: someone new to the job or new to the school will need extra support
- the activity: library activities should be low risk
- the facilities: library facilities should be safe
- the location: the location should be safe and close to help if there is a problem.

Therefore, **CILIP recommends that**:

- **the librarian have support in the library, particularly at break and lunchtimes**
- **all out-of-school hours use be properly supervised**
- **fire inspections and insurance cover, both for physical safety and for the number of students who can be safely supervised, reflect out-of-school hours use**
- **proper emergency and evacuation procedures be in place**
- **the library be included in rotas for senior management duty cover**
- **the librarian be included in arrangements for disciplinary codes and procedures as well as the whole-school reward system**
- **the librarian have the status and authority to exercise behaviour management strategies in the school library, in line with school policies.**

Management of ICT

As the use of ICT expands in all areas of teaching and learning, librarians must be prepared to re-think their roles and re-define the traditional library. ICT is a hugely motivating tool, and can engage students with learning, attitudinal and language difficulties. It can also extend the learning experience of all students, not just those who are gifted and talented. Librarians need to embrace ICT, participate in all that it offers to students and teachers, and recognize how it inspires independent learning. All school librarians have a responsibility to foster the effective use of ICT through the selection of appropriate resources, and through the teaching of skills to enable effective student use of the new technologies.

Librarians can make an important contribution to the development of the school's intranet and website. The intranet should be a marketing tool for library services, activities and resources, as well as an information tool. Many school librarians have taken on the responsibility for intranet development across their whole schools. This is a natural development for the school's information specialist, and can demonstrate and affirm the central role of the librarian as the school's knowledge manager.

Virtual learning environments (VLEs) and managed learning environments (MLEs) are currently under development and are being used in a number of schools in a variety of ways (see Appendix 6). The development of broadband technology through the National Grid for Learning has provided high speed internet connectivity for local authority schools, although access to personal computers or laptops can still be a limiting factor for individual students and staff. School librarians need to apprise themselves of the infrastructure and connectivity issues in their schools, and identify the areas where they can best contribute. Options will include:

- managing the school's internal intranet for effective internal communication
- designing and managing the school's external website
- being part of any VLE development to ensure seamless access to the library's resources
- providing links to the National Grid for Learning and the Virtual Teacher Centre[5]
- organizing the school's internet 'favourites' or 'bookmarks'
- ensuring that the library catalogue is accessible over the intranet or any wider area network (WAN) developed by the school, such as a VLE or MLE
- providing links from library internet computers or the library pages on the school intranet to bookmarked sites to support specific areas of work
- providing website reviews for staff and students
- developing interactive pages on the school's intranet to promote reading and useful resources and library activities and services
- contributing to the school's daily news items on the intranet
- arranging subscriptions to appropriate online services as an alternative to purchasing hard copy stock
- providing details and advice for the school on 'superhighway safety' and copyright issues[6-8]

Chapter 3 The management of the school library **19**

- keeping up to date with web-based developments in their library management systems that will enhance accessibility of resources where either a VLE or an MLE is planned.
- becoming an expert in ICT authoring tools, both for publishing library-related information, and assisting students and teachers in developing web-based presentations and e-learning resources.

The following are further issues for which the librarian needs to take responsibility within the management of ICT.

Stock

A school's management team might perceive that the ready availability of professionally produced electronic learning materials and a plethora of websites challenge the prevailing concept of a school library, and thereby conclude that less money should to be spent on print resources and the library as a whole. There is no evidence to suggest that the end of the book is in sight and the librarian must build a strong case for the continuing spend on books, citing:

- issues of differentiation
- the value of print versus online information in specific situations and the development of selection skills
- access: this will always be an issue until there is a computer available to every student no matter where he/she is, in or out of school
- reader development: the vital role of the library in developing readers must not be undermined or diminished by a lack of resources.

Within the area of resource provision, librarians need to develop the role of knowledge manager. They should be familiar with online resources as well as other e-learning products and be able to assist teachers in selecting the ones that will enhance their lessons, along with the print resources located physically in the library. Such a role is necessary to find a route through the information overload that teachers suffer owing to the rapid growth of electronic materials.

Materials fund

- More will need to be spent on subscriptions for e-learning materials, but where these are being made available across the school network or via a broadband or VLE, as they all should be, the money should come from central funds and not the library budget.
- The library budget can therefore be reduced by the value of its existing online subscriptions, but the book fund should not be reduced.

Staff

- All library staff need to be skilled to ECDL (European Computer Driving Licence) or equivalent level.
- Librarians need CPD that focuses on:
  - new technological developments
  - issues and skills surrounding teaching and learning with electronic resources
  - strategies for effective implementation of library services through VLEs or MLEs, where these are developing
- Librarians should be participating in the delivery of INSET sessions for teachers on the effective use of electronic content to maximize learning outcomes.

Information literacy and e-learning

- The skills of information literacy should be supported through any electronic lesson delivery of curriculum subjects.
- If generic information literacy offerings are developed, they should be designed so that they can be easily customized for subject-specific application.
- The librarian is the key person to act as instigator, developer and partner in the delivery of information literacy skills across the curriculum.

Hardware and space

- There needs to be a careful design of available space, which allows for increased computer hardware, but not to the detriment of other services (resources and study space).
- Hardware that is space efficient and does not impede multi-format (print and electronic) use or group learning should be given serious consideration.
- A budget for the replacement cycle of machines should be secure.

References

1 Birmingham Schools Library Service, *The Difference We're Making: library provision in Birmingham secondary schools*, Birmingham Advisory and Support Service, 2002.
2 Williams, D., Wavell, C. and Coles, L., *Impact of School Library Services on Achievement and Learning: critical literature review*, The Robert Gordon University, 2001, www.resource.gov.uk/documents/impactsl.pdf.
3 Sheffield Hallam University, *Survey of Secondary School Libraries: a report prepared for CILIP*, October, 2002, www.cilip.org.uk/practice/ssl.html.
4 NVQ, www.dfes.gov.uk/nvq/.

5 *Virtual Teacher Centre*, http://vtc.ngfl.gov.uk/docserver.php.
6 *Superhighway Safety: safe use of the internet*, DfES, www.safety.ngfl.gov.uk.
7 Libraries and Archives Copyright Alliance,
   www.cilip.org.uk/committees/laca/laca.html
8 Norman, S. (2004) *Practical Copyright for Information Professionals: the CILIP handbook*, London, Facet Publishing.

Useful links for CPD

American Association of School Librarians (AASL)
   www.ala.org/aasl/
Australian School Library Association (ASLA)
   www.asla.org.au
Chartered Institute of Library and Information Professionals (CILIP)
   www.cilip.org.uk/
Education Libraries Group
   www.cilip.org.uk/groups/elg/
International Association of School Librarianship: School Libraries Online
   www.iasl-slo.org/
School Library Association (SLA)
   www.sla.org.uk/
School Librarians Group (SLG)
   www.cilip.org.uk/groups/slg/slg.html
Strongest Links: The Website for UK School Librarians
   www.strongest-links.org.uk/

Discussion lists

School Librarians' Network
   To subscribe send an email with 'Subscribe' in the subject to:
   sln-subscribe@yahoogroups.com.
LIS-EDUC: Library Services for Education
   To join lis-educ, send an e-mail message to jiscmail@jiscmail.ac.uk with the command: join lis-educ *firstname lastname*.

4

Facilities management

CILIP recommends that the physical environment of the school library should support its role as a whole-school learning resource at the heart of the school community.

Libraries should actively involve young people in the design of the services offered to them, not as a one-off or ad hoc gesture, but as an ongoing process.
Recommendation 8.4, *Start with the Child*[1]

The design and layout of the library will set the tone for the environment and the ethos of the facility and contribute to the positive experiences of all users: students, staff and the whole school community. As one of the major learning spaces within a school, it must seek out and respond to the needs of all user groups. This chapter will look at the following areas, all of which need consideration when planning and managing the library facility:

- function and environment
- location and use
- space requirements
- signage
- display.

The checklist in Appendix 7 addresses further practical considerations. It is

The CILIP Guidelines for Secondary School Libraries

intended to be a tool to help librarians identify the strengths and weaknesses in their existing facilities and plan for improvements.

Regardless of the existing space and position of the school library, the majority of general principles outlined here can be applied and are certainly important in planning any new development. Schools library services provide an independent, unbiased source of advice and support in developing effective and well planned library facilities in schools, and should be involved in any new development. Throughout the chapter, cognizance has been taken of the implications of the Special Educational Needs and Disability Act 2001.[2]

Function and environment

A library is a learning space, and the planning and design must focus on this as its principal purpose. As it must support the whole school community, flexibility needs to be built in to stimulate multiple intelligences and accommodate a range of learning styles. The work of learning theorists such as Howard Gardner[3] and Barbara Prashnig[4] has highlighted how environment interacts with different learning styles. Everyone has a unique thinking, working and learning style, and as the heart of learning in the school, the library should offer something for everyone. Often this requires a minimum of rearranging or investment and will pay dividends, not only in increased productivity and enhanced learning, but also in improved behaviour and positive attitudes to reading for life. The following are some suggestions to consider.

- **Work area**
  The work area should be carefully zoned and clearly signed with informal areas for those who need them. Research shows that many people learn best on beanbags, cushions or sprawled on rugs on the floor, others prefer more formal furniture – hard seating and study tables or carrels – or an informal café style learning space with low level tables and easy chairs or sofas. People's preference for working independently varies too – some prefer pair-sharing while others need the stimulation of a team. Flexible furniture will allow for all these different sociability groupings. Similarly, other learners need space to walk about to think clearly and creatively.
- **Lighting**
  The level of lighting also affects how students perform. Bright light makes some learners restless and fidgety while others find that low light has a calming effect and enables them to think more clearly. Different effects can be created with careful positioning of spotlights or wall-mounted light-fittings.
- **Noise**
  Many students, particularly in secondary schools, need music or noisy environments to think and remember better. Conversely, there will always be

some students who need near silence to concentrate and work effectively. The learning environment of the library should cater for all, perhaps with a sound system for soft background music for downtime and reflection or listening posts and portable CD players which can be used both by more analytic learners to block out other noise and by auditory learners needing music to aid concentration. Alternatively, consider having quiet times advertised during the day. It is worth researching the effects of music on learning, as the wrong kind can destroy learning even for auditory learners. Used correctly it can aid information intake and processing, spark connections, stimulate the imagination, reduce brain stress, integrate both sides of the brain and create that state of 'relaxed alertness' vital for learning to happen. Mozart, Vivaldi and rhythmic baroque music are all recommended. Students for whom noise is important will often need to talk and discuss with other learners.

- **Eating and drinking**
  Many students concentrate better when snacking or drinking while others find it inhibits the learning process. It may be necessary to be flexible with the traditional 'library rules'. A constant supply of water enables the brain to make more and better connections and improves memory. Serious thought should be given to installing cool water dispensers.

- **Heating**
  Heating may be something over which one has little control. Since some learners need warmth in order to study while others prefer cool temperatures, it is vital to ensure that your learning environment is adequately ventilated.

- **Movement**
  Tactile or kinaesthetic learners need to fiddle, doodle or constantly handle objects in order to relax, focus concentration, process new information and stimulate brain activity. It is worth planning a creativity or modelling corner stocked with paper, flipchart, markers, colours, card, etc. where they can experiment and try out their learning or an ideas board for large-scale doodling and playing with ideas.

- **Colour**
  Careful thought needs to be given to colour choices and combinations. Interior design and colour theory suggest that yellow inspires creativity, blue aids reflection, green calms, and purple promotes memory retention, while reds and hot oranges overstimulate and encourage aggression and bad behaviour!

  If full-scale redecoration is impossible, colour can be introduced through noticeboards. Display is very important to visual learners. Brightly coloured display boards can be used not only to showcase outstanding student work, but also as an interactive resource:

  − A scribble board can be used for posing questions, suggesting answers and

putting forward ideas for discussion.
- A 'big questions' board to encourage new thinking can be provided.
- An ideas board for items in the news, topic keywords or new resources can be provided or a thought-board displaying positive learning messages and quotations.
- This 'science of suggestion' is well proven. The suggestopedic approach relaxes students, makes learning fun and bypasses common barriers to learning. Many libraries also make use of interactive whiteboards to display scrolling tickertape-type positive learning messages to stimulate new thinking and learning and encourage good questioning skills.
- Because of the way the brain works posters displayed above eye-level to the left aid information recall while to the right they inspire creative thinking. Similarly red against green display should be avoided since it creates difficulties for large numbers of colour-blind students.

The aim, then, in rethinking any learning environment and planning an appropriate space is to cater for individual learning needs. Small things can make a very big difference. School libraries are beginning to respond to this challenge imaginatively. Examples may be found in the work of initiatives such as the University of the First Age,[5] and the Accelerated Learning Initiative,[6] which link recent brain research to learning provision in schools.

A positive learning ethos is crucial for a library to achieve its optimum contribution to the school. This ethos cannot be achieved where the library is timetabled for use as an ordinary classroom, or negatively used as a detention area, a sixth form social area, or a place to send badly behaved, unsupervised students. There is a need to create a design that actively promotes a learning ethos for all students and an attractive, welcoming environment plays a large part in making the library a valued and well-used part of the school. Involving students in the design and furnishing of the library can be a powerful way of encouraging their ownership and pride in the facility.

The issue desk has long been accepted as an essential focal point in the school library. However, it can be imposing and it separates the library staff from the users. Librarians should consider whether the traditional model is still useful, particularly in situations where self-issue systems are installed or being considered. Whatever configuration is decided upon, be it a multifunctional desk that includes space for administrative activities, or just a low enquiry point, it is essential that the design and height do not impair access for users with disabilities or present a barrier to effective interaction with any user.

Location and use

It has now become widely accepted that access to a large range of resources is crucial to the teaching and learning programmes of all departments. Classes will book in regularly to do research with print and electronic resources, and information literacy skills will be taught. Individuals and small groups will drop in to find information or reading material or to pursue a variety of independent learning activities. Even larger numbers of students will use the library to do their homework, to read, and to find material to further their own individual interests before and after school and at break and lunch times.

The location of the library has an impact on facilitating its use. While in most cases the location is pre-determined, where new developments are planned or where relocation opportunities arise, the following principles should be taken into account.

- The library should be on one floor only, preferably the ground floor, to enable good access for disabled users and easy delivery of goods. Where dual school/community use is planned, especially out of school hours, a ground floor location close to an external entrance is essential for security reasons.
- The library should be centrally sited within the school, close to the maximum number of teaching areas, though not a thoroughfare. An isolated location or separate building will deter regular use. This is backed up by recent research by Opening the Book that shows that library usage decreased significantly when the library was located on the second floor of a building.[7]

Space requirements

The DfES has made recommendations on space for school libraries in *Area Guidelines for Schools* and is in the process of updating these. At the time of writing a summary of the planned changes is available on the internet.[8] The *Guidelines* make recommendations for 'learning resource areas' and recognize that the single largest element of these will be the school library. They also recommend that school libraries should be able to seat 10% of a school's students at any one time. In addition, there should be adequate space for library materials, furniture, equipment and administrative accommodation.

The evolution of the school library at the heart of the curriculum places additional demands on space and facilities:

- Departmental collections are discouraged in favour of a central resource available to all.
- Collaborative working is now the norm and study table spaces need to be generous enough to accommodate this.
- The importance of electronic resources means that there needs to be sufficient space for students to lay out books and other resources, to work together and to take notes while using workstations.

The CILIP Guidelines for Secondary School Libraries

- Careers information should be provided in the library for central, open access with adequate space and shelving to accommodate the variety of formats.

The requirement for administrative/office space should not be overlooked. It should include storage space, shelving, staff desk(s) and computer(s), and a filing cabinet and work area for processing new acquisitions, and it should have a good visual overview of the library.

The space recommended in the revised *Area Guidelines* falls short of what is needed in order to meet all of these requirements. On the principle that the library is a centralized learning resource that is fully integrated into the life of the educational institution, CILIP recommends that the space provision should not be less than that recommended for all learning resource areas within a school. This is supported by the much more generous recommendations of the Further Educational Funding Council (FEFC) for the amount of space required to provide effective learning resource areas to support independent learning in Sixth Form Colleges.[9] The first column in the sliding scale of space given in Table 4.1 is CILIP's recommendation for library space in relation to student populations in 11–16 secondary schools. The second column shows an increased figure reflecting the additional space required when that population includes a post-16 cohort.

Table 4.1 Library space

Students	Library accommodation, m^2	
	Min.	Max.
800	340	370
900	370	400
1000	400	440
1100	440	475
1200	470	510
1300	500	550
1400	535	580
1500	570	620

Signage

Good signage is essential both inside and outside the library, including clear signposting from other parts of the school. Students should be consulted as to the types of signs needed to guide them to the locations and resources they need.

Within the library there should be:

- a plan of the library layout
- a bay or ceiling and shelf guides to indicate non-fiction subjects and fiction

genre or author areas
- a subject index in poster format that leads into full subject access through the library catalogue
- guidelines and notices about the use of the library, including copyright and acceptable behaviour.

Notices should be phrased positively (e.g. 'Please take your food and snacks to the areas of the school where eating is allowed' rather than 'Please don't eat or drink in the library').

All main signs should be pictorial with a minimum of text so as not to exclude students with special needs. Consideration should be given to signs in community languages as well. All signs should be designed with clarity for external visitors and for people with physical, including visual, disabilities.[10-12]

Display

Display is not only a powerful tool for the promotion of library resources, services and activities but also for enhancing the literacy of students and stimulating their intellectual curiosity. Everything should be designed with this in mind. Displays should always be up to date, often designed in collaboration with students and possibly focused on some of the following:

- students' work resulting from library activities such as book reviews and projects
- promotion and information about new acquisitions
- resources on chosen themes/interests
- stories in the news linked to relevant library resources
- careers information
- general information about events and activities in the library, the school and the local community.

Display systems are available from all major library and school suppliers. Some of these include:

- wall-mounted and portable display boards
- leaflet dispensers and book stands
- end display panels for shelving units.

Alternatively, card-based display board (e.g. Kappa-board) can be purchased locally from specialist art suppliers, cut to size and painted or covered with paper to provide attractive backgrounds for displays.

References

1 Chartered Institute of Library and Information Professionals, *Start with the Child: report of the CILIP working group on library provision for children and young people*, CILIP, 2002, www.cilip.org.uk/advocacy/startwiththechild/startwiththechild.pdf.

2 Special Educational Needs and Disability Act 2001, The Stationery Office Ltd, www.hmso.gov.uk/acts/acts2001/20010010.htm.

3 Gardner, H., *Frames of Mind*, New York, Basic Books, 1985.

4 Prashnig, B., *The Power of Diversity*, David Bateman Ltd, 1998.

5 University of the First Age, www.ufa.org.uk/.

6 Accelerated Learning in Training and Education, www.alite.co.uk.

7 Van Riel, R., Getting Past G, *Library & Information Update*, (August), 2002, 38–9.

8 *Area Guidelines for Schools* (draft), www.teachernet.gov.uk/sbareaguidelines, Section 4, 24–8.

9 *Guidance on Floorspace Management in Further Education Colleges: supplement to Circular 97/37*, FEFC, 1997, http://lsc.wwt.co.uk/documents/circulars/fefc_pubs/9737s.pdf.

10 Special Educational Needs and Disability Act 2001, The Stationery Office Ltd, www.hmso.gov.uk/acts/acts2001/20010010.htm.

11 www.bda-dyslexia.org.uk.

12 Resource, *Library Services for Visually Impaired People, A Manual of Best Practice,* http://bpm.nlb-online.org/.

5

Management of learning resources

CILIP recommends that the school support the vital role that quality resources play in stimulating learning with recommended levels of investment (providing 13 items per student) and that it seek to maximize the impact of this investment by managing resources centrally.

Access to services and collections should be based on the United Nations Universal Declaration of Human Rights and Freedoms, and should not be subject to any form of ideological, political or religious censorship, or to commercial pressures.
The School Library Manifesto[1]

The complexity of managing learning resources has grown considerably in the last decade with the influx of electronic information and e-resources available in schools. This chapter offers guidance on managing this growth by examining the issues of:

- location
- needs assessment
- selection
- organization and access
- budgeting.

The current context for managing learning resources is characterized by:

The CILIP Guidelines for Secondary School Libraries

- an emphasis on independent learning
- the unique contribution of reader development
- the use of ICT as a tool for teaching and learning
- the key importance of information literacy
- the growing importance of e-learning and the development of intranets, broadband services and virtual learning environments (VLEs)
- increased understanding of how the brain works – the physiology of learning.

The best and most useful resources will to appeal to individual students – inspiring an enthusiasm to learn, stimulating curiosity and suiting a variety of learning styles. Students should enjoy using the library's resources. They need to see their own interests and cultures reflected and validated by inclusion in the school library.

This means that the secondary school library must contain a full range of imaginative fiction, from picture books to novels, and the widest possible non-fiction range. It needs to include representations of different life styles, cultures (including youth culture) and faiths. Resources need to relate directly to curriculum needs to support and sustain students' achievement. Access to electronic resources needs to be integrated with books, recordings and resources provided in other media. The richer the resource base, the richer the learning experience of students.

Librarians need to be clear about the resource implications of these demands, ensure that they are understood by senior management, financed accordingly, and that the human resources necessary to manage them effectively are in place.

Location

- Students and staff need access to the widest possible range of resources in one location.
- The school network and the internet need to be available in the library with access sufficient for at least half a class to use at any one time.
- The establishment of pocket collections in departments may result in high levels of loss and costly duplications between departments. Resources that are located in departments should be recorded on the library management system for ease of location, to facilitate use by the whole school and to enable departmental stock checking.

Needs assessment

In order to build a relevant resource base for the whole school community, librarians need to be involved in a continuous process of needs assessment, comparing changing demands to available resources. This process forms the foundation for planning collection development and budget requests. In brief,

Chapter 5 Management of learning resources

librarians need to:

- be familiar with the physical, emotional and moral issues facing young people and manage resources relating to these issues in a supportive way
- be aware of issues of cultural diversity both within the school and in the wider community
- maintain a constant awareness of curriculum changes and developments both internally and in the national arena
- involve students and staff by encouraging them to identify stock gaps and recommend purchases
- have a knowledge of how access can be provided to learning resources for school library users who have special needs or who are disabled
- have knowledge of and be able to assess resources available from external sources such as the schools library service, local public libraries, museums and archives, and the British Library; be able to judge the cost effectiveness of accessing these resources in relation to the demand within the school
- carry out annual stock checks and regular reviews and evaluation of stock, including purchased online resources, to measure relevance to existing demands and to plan for future developments.

Selection

The key responsibility of the librarian is to meet identified needs with quality information and fiction resources. This depends on good communication between librarians and all sectors of the school population as well as the librarian's professional knowledge of the curriculum, publishing, and external sources of information.

There should be a written resource policy that covers:

- whole-school ethos and policies
- a commitment to culturally diverse stock
- criteria for the identification and selection of books, multimedia and e-resources, including internet sites made accessible through the library system, or the school's intranet or virtual learning environment (VLE)
- materials meeting the curricular and extra-curricular needs of students
- materials that promote reading for pleasure
- materials reflecting curriculum development
- materials covering leisure interests
- materials in alternative formats that are accessible to visually impaired library users and those with other special needs
- differentiated materials in a variety of formats appropriate to the ability range and interests of the students, enabling access and stimulation for all

- materials balanced to avoid sexist, cultural, political, ethical or homophobic bias
- materials reflecting current youth culture and concerns
- materials in community languages
- a focus on the inclusion of current, accurate and authoritative materials
- an appropriate balance between fiction and non-fiction
- clear procedures for handling complaints.

Aids to selection

Aids to selection include:

- encouraging students to participate in selection and to offer comments and suggestions
- enabling students to help with stock selection through shop and library supplier visits, by using the internet and by accessing review magazines
- keeping up to date with quality, unbiased, critical information about new resources across all formats in the professional press and on the internet
- accessing the expertise of schools library services staff for advice and information about the latest publications
- attending exhibitions of resources held at major library suppliers and schools library services
- encouraging students and/or members of the community with special language skills to participate in the selection of materials in these languages
- visiting publishers' displays at major library and education exhibitions
- taking advantage of visits from publishers' representatives or booksellers, bearing in mind that it is important to ensure that any 'bargain' boxes of books are good value for money and really do meet the library's most pressing stock gap needs.

Organization and access

While libraries need to be orderly and systematic, they also need to be flexible in the presentation of materials. Children learn in different ways and the emphasis should be on how students will be drawn to resources and how they will use them. Providing clear, unfettered access to a collection is the single most important factor in maximizing its effectiveness and stimulating use. Generally speaking, this will mean:

- organizing non-fiction using the Dewey Decimal System
- ordering fiction by genre or author
- allowing for flexibility in order to spark interest as part of a promotion or to make materials more accessible in a particular local situation

Chapter 5 Management of learning resources **35**

- comprehensive and accurate keywording of all materials, including internet sites and other e-resources, in the library management system, which will lead students directly to resources, regardless of location, and encourage them to value all types of sources in their research; this includes linking resource access via the library pages on the school's intranet or VLE
- printed subject indexes in the form of posters, directional signage or leaflets and bookmarks, that point students quickly to a general section and which may form part of the library's promotion and display
- central recording of all learning resources in the school in the library management system, which enables staff and students to have easy access to materials located in departments and provides for cost effective measures to be taken, such as textbook issues and departmental stock checks.

The library should also include certain special collections where appropriate, such as:

- careers information
- professional resources for staff
- local history and information.

Resources budget

The annual library development plan is the appropriate place to highlight collection development needs and the financial commitment required to meet them. Details of development planning are to be found in Chapter 2 and helpful steps are also in the *Empowerment Pack for School Libraries*.[2] The development of bids for resources funding is also detailed in the Empowerment Pack and should include the following:

- liaison with curriculum managers and subject teachers to determine curriculum needs and changes
- consultation with senior management to identify whole-school priorities
- inclusion of online subscriptions (needs and costs)
- rationale for funding online resources for whole school use from central funds rather than library budgets
- monitoring of student and teacher needs via suggestions, surveys, and statistics of use for all formats
- reviewing stock to plan for filling gaps and replacing outdated and worn materials
- comparison of current stock against recommended levels
- implications of OFSTED or other inspection reports
- review of schools library service provision and the appropriate level of support

- calculation of costs of proposals based on current average unit costs, student numbers, recommended stock figures and inflation, obsolescence, withdrawal and replacement
- regular cogent, well supported and documented presentations to senior management.

The budget bid will need to be submitted to senior management and/or to the Governors at an appropriate time of year. The librarian's role is to clarify with senior management what procedure is best in the particular school, and to discuss this with their line manager. It will also be helpful to discuss the budget process with the school bursar or business manager.

Recommended figures for library resourcing

CILIP recommends that:

Libraries stock a minimum of 13 items per student for the 11–16 age range. An appropriate figure for post-16 would be 17 items per student, as recommended in *Guidelines for Learning Resource Services in Further and Higher Education*.[3]

The recommended ratio of fiction to non-fiction is 1:4 or 1:5, depending on the priorities of the school and the school library.

It is also recommended that 10% of the library stock be replaced annually, which reflects the need for stock to be in good condition, relevant and up to date.

The above figures encompass all areas of library stock – books, electronic resources, periodical and newspaper subscriptions, etc.

Average cost per item prices are available from the Booktrust's website,[4] the Publishers' Association[5] and schools library services.

References

1 IFLA/UNESCO, *The School Library Manifesto*, IFLA, 2000, www.ifla.org/VII/s11/pubs/manifest.htm.
2 *Empowerment Pack for School Libraries*, www.cilip.org.uk/advocacy/empowerment.html.
3 Ennis, K. (ed.), *Guidelines for Learning Resource Services in Further and Higher Education*, Library Association Publishing, 2000.
4 Booktrust, www.booktrust.org.uk.
5 Booktrust, *Recommended Spending on Books in Schools: Booktrust Research Report*, January, 2002, www.publishers.org.uk/paweb/paweb.nsf/pubframe!Open.

6

Information literacy

> CILIP recommends that the school commit itself to the development of information-literate students who are able to become independent, lifelong learners, and sees the librarian taking a lead role in this development.

Participation in the information society requires the citizen to be information literate. Failure to appraise information and a lack of confidence in the use of information, in whatever format, will result in exclusion. Libraries have a key role to play in its development.

Start with the Child, 2002[1]

Information literacy can be described as 'the ability to locate pertinent information, evaluate its reliability, analyse and synthesise the information to construct personal meaning, and apply it to informed decision making'.[2]

Information literacy is the key to successful information use by students. It is through the teaching and learning of information-literacy skills that students will gain confidence in using the full range of library and information resources they need for formal education, for lifelong learning, and for participation in society generally.

Information-literacy skills

In order to handle and process information successfully, students need to be able to:

- **Question**. Identify a problem, establish what is already known and frame questions around what is not known[3] (see examples in Appendix 8).
- **Plan**. Devise a plan for taking enquiries forward and completing a research task.
- **Identify and evaluate sources**. Establish appropriate search strategies, identify appropriate sources of information and analyse and evaluate the information found.[4,5]
- **Analyse and organize key information**. Compare and contrast information identifying key ideas and concepts and make appropriate notes and records using a variety of techniques. Discard what is not needed, organize the relevant information and document sources.
- **Synthesize and assimilate**. Combine relevant information from a variety of sources into a new whole. Compare with what was already known and assimilate new understandings/decisions (for helpful electronic tools see Filamentality[6] and Webquests[7]).
- **Reflect**. Revisit questions and test for any gaps to see if supporting information is sufficient to enable a conclusion to be drawn or a decision to be made.
- **Communicate**. Communicate the new learning or the conclusion to the intended audience in an appropriate way, with insight, detail and accuracy in an effective, original presentation.
- **Evaluate**. Evaluate the final product and the whole learning process to complete the task, drawing conclusions about what has been learned and the effectiveness of the process.

The need for these skills is not new. Benjamin Bloom identified them in his Taxonomy in 1956,[8] where the differentiation between lower order cognitive skills (knowledge, comprehension, application) and higher order cognitive skills (analysis, synthesis, evaluation) is articulated. In 1984 Michael Marland developed his 9 Question Steps[9] from which further models evolved in the 1980s and 1990s. Some widely used ones are Mike Eisenberg's The Big 6,[10] James Herring's PLUS Model[11] and David Wray's Exit Model.[12] There is now an imperative within new curricula to develop the higher order skills in a much wider context than before, with an increasingly wide range of resources. This takes the work that school librarians do with teaching and learning much further than in the past.

Information-literacy skills, like all other skills, have the most impact on learning when they are taught, modelled and practised within a meaningful context. Ideally these skills will be introduced in a developmental progression beginning at pre-school, continuing throughout formal education and translating into lifelong learning. In order for this to happen, each step must be carefully coached and supported, as well as differentiated by age and ability levels. It is also important that these steps are seen as a cyclical rather than a linear process in which students reflect upon and refine their strategies as they question, analyse, assimilate, evaluate, conclude, and learn.

Developing the provision of information literacy skills

The best way forward is to develop, through consultation with staff, a method that is based on existing skills and needs, that relates to the school development plan and incorporates recognized models of good practice. It is helpful to remember that real change and development take time and that the process should not be rushed nor should there be expectations of immediate success with the whole school. The following are strategies that a school, led by the librarian, may consider when planning and developing an information-literacy skills curriculum:

1   Identify people who are interested in learning how the incorporation of information-literacy skills into their curricula can enhance students' ability to learn in their subjects.
2   Develop methods for teaching the relevant skills in a curricular context, working with teachers across a variety of subjects and key stages, as pilot projects.
3   Monitor and evaluate student progress and attainment both in terms of information literacy and subject knowledge – developing case studies where appropriate to build a bank of evidence-based practice that can be shared and used for advocacy.
4   Evaluate and refine the pilot projects.
5   Disseminate examples of good practice through presentations to senior management and the whole staff through departmental meetings, INSET sessions and individual communications with critical friends.
6   Over time, monitor information literacy skills development and student progression across subjects and age ranges to provide a spiralling IL curriculum (see Figure 6.1) where students revisit skills in different contexts at increasing levels of sophistication throughout their school career.

The educational imperative

The planning group will also need to be involved in creating an environment in which information literacy becomes an integral part of the teaching and learning in all departments. Everyone in the school (governors, senior staff, teaching staff, support staff, students, parents) should be made aware of the educational value of information literacy as a key component in:

• raising achievement
• developing critical thinking skills

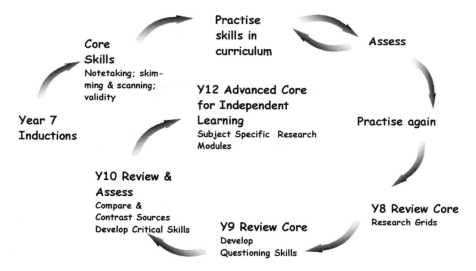

Figure 6.1 The spiralling curriculum

- developing lifelong learning skills
- raising literacy standards
- providing for differentiation
- developing effective use of ICT
- delivering national curricula.

The following sections outline some of the points to be highlighted during the development of information literacy across the curriculum.

- **Raising achievement**
  Information-literacy skills teaching has been shown to contribute to raising achievement:
    - a number of studies in the USA have shown a link between attainment and well developed school library media programmes that are led by professional librarians[13]
    - a review of UK and international research has shown that school libraries can have a positive impact on academic achievement.[14]
- **Information-literacy skills teaching develops critical thinking by:**
    - developing questioning skills that are needed to determine what is already known and what one needs to find out
    - developing the ability to identify key words, information and concepts
    - developing the ability to evaluate information in all formats for validity and relevance, bias, etc.

Chapter 6 Information literacy

- developing the ability to compare, contrast and synthesize relevant information
- developing the ability to present information in an appropriate format for purpose and audience.
- **Information-literacy skills teaching encourages lifelong learning by:**
  - developing a confidence with information that will stimulate a desire to learn and placing students in control of their own learning
  - developing the cognitive skills needed for problem solving, which are transferable to any future learning experience
  - developing research expertise, which students will need to find information to update their skills or knowledge at any time
  - developing skills that are not dependent on any particular library or resource but are transferable to any type of information
  - enabling learners to be self-organizing, independent and self-critical of their learning
  - providing learners with opportunities to develop alternative strategies for learning that can be tailored to individual needs
  - contributing to individuals' ability to make assessments and choices for leisure reading.
- **Information-literacy skills teaching raises literacy standards by:**
  - developing critical reading skills (reading for a purpose) using a variety of information resources
  - embedding different reading strategies (skimming, scanning, intensive reading)
  - developing the individual's ability to be able to choose the appropriate strategy for a given purpose
  - enabling students to become effective users of information in a variety of formats.
- **Information-literacy skills teaching provides for differentiation through:**
  - the use of a large range of resources that cater for different abilities and learning situations
  - learning opportunities that assist children in determining their own preferred learning styles and strategies and expanding their own portfolio of styles
  - providing staff with strategies for differentiating assignments and learning outcomes.
- **Information-literacy skills teaching develops the effective use of ICT by:**
  - ensuring that individuals are able to take effective advantage of information and communication technologies
  - providing students with the ability to use ICT as one of a range of possible resources, by understanding the purpose at hand and the appropriateness

of different types of sources
- developing critical skills to interact with information and ideas, so as to enable individuals to make efficient and appropriate use of the vast amounts of electronic information available (e.g. learning how to evaluate and select information from resources with limited structure and no quality control)
- providing students with the facility to update their skills and knowledge to enable them to cope with the rapid change brought about by technological developments.
- **Information-literacy skills teaching contributes to the delivery of national curricula by:**
  - providing opportunities for students to use a range of resources, and to develop analytical and critical thinking skills and the ability to reflect on their learning
  - ensuring that students have the information handling skills to manage their learning within and beyond the requirements of national curricula.

Responsibility for implementing information literacy skills

Senior management, the curriculum manager, the librarian, other key teaching staff and the schools library service all have a role to play in providing successful and appropriate information literacy skills training within the school, as described below.

- **Senior management and the curriculum manager will:**
  - ensure that the librarian has the time, support, training and status to enable him/her to work with teaching colleagues to develop curricular opportunities for information-literacy teaching and learning
  - ensure that the development of the library, its resources, and its role in teaching and learning within the school is part of the development and planning process of the school.
- **Librarians will:**
  - be involved with the school's curriculum development planning and provide a base of resources to meet its needs
  - be aware of key educational initiatives and their impact on teaching and learning
  - be familiar with and apply the principles and practice of good teaching, including teaching to clear objectives and outcomes, interactive teaching and learning styles, developing thinking skills, and modelling[15,16]
  - be familiar with accelerated learning styles[17,18] and current brain-based research[19] to enable better communication with teaching colleagues and develop practical strategies that help students learn

Chapter 6 Information literacy

- maintain an overview of information literacy development within the school
- provide stimulus and support for further developments in information literacy within the school
- provide staff INSET sessions and expertise to assist teaching staff in embedding information literacy in the curriculum and in assessing students' progress.
- **Teachers will:**
  - provide the curricular context for skills teaching
  - work together with the librarian in planning, differentiating, implementing, and evaluating information literacy teaching embedded in their subjects
  - use a variety of teaching and learning strategies to provide students with opportunities to practise information literacy skills.
- **Schools library services and other professional organizations will:**
  - assist schools to recruit appropriately qualified (i.e. Chartered) librarians who can provide the necessary expertise to collaborate in information literacy development
  - provide authority-wide INSET for librarians, teachers, and senior management on information literacy
  - support information literacy by offering access to a wide range of differentiated resources through a project loan service
  - advise on strategies for developing information skills practice within the school.

Factors in successful development of information literacy in the school curriculum

- A librarian with the status, support, training, skills and time to be a driving force for information literacy within the school.
- Strong whole-school, senior management support for the development of independent learning and information literacy development within the school.
- Co-operation between the librarian and teaching colleagues in the identification, planning, teaching and assessing of information literacy skills within the school.
- An accessible and up-to-date collection of a range of resources, including books, periodicals, newspapers, CD-ROMs, online information, etc., that both require and enable students to develop and practise their information literacy skills.
- Ongoing evaluation of the school's effectiveness in the teaching and learning of information literacy.

The information-literacy curriculum is a developmental one that contributes to school effectiveness. It is implemented through good school management, communication, curriculum development and partnerships between all those involved in the teaching and learning process. The information-literacy curriculum may therefore be regarded as an example of value-added education and enhances educational opportunities for all.

Useful resources

Dubber, G., *Developing Information Skills Through the Secondary School Library*, School Library Association, 1999.

www.leeds.ac.uk/bigblue/

Big Blue project in information skills for HE and post-16 students, based at Leeds University.

www.sconul.ac.uk/activities/inf_lit/papers/Seven_pillars2.pdf

Sconul's briefing paper on information skills in higher education, popularly known as the Seven Pillars Project.

www.warwick.ac.uk/staff/D.J.Wray/resources.html

David Wray of Warwick University has written extensively on teaching literacy particularly on the use of writing frames in non-fiction writing.

www.fno.org/

Jamie McKenzie of the USA has developed ways of using information literacy skills to enhance the use of technology in schools. This website introduces his ideas through articles and links to his books.

www.big6.com/

The Big 6 is an American model for teaching information literacy, which has influenced the teaching of these skills throughout the world.

http://jimmy.qmuc.ac.uk/usr/jherri/plus/default.htm

James Herring, then of Queen Margaret University College, Edinburgh, adapted the Big 6 to create a model of information literacy known as PLUS

www.sldirectory.com/libsf/resf/infoskill.html

Gwen Gawaith who originally published the very useful *Library Alive* has developed new methods for delivering information literacy. She publishes an online newsletter from New Zealand that includes examples of good practice from several countries.

References

1 Chartered Institute of Library and Information Professionals, *Start with the Child: report of the CILIP working group on library provision for children and young people*, CILIP, 2002, www.cilip.org.uk/advocacy/startwiththechild/startwiththechild.pdf.

2 Berger, P., *Internet for Active Learners*, American Library Association (out of print).

3 Inspiration, www.inspiration.com.

4 Quick, www.quick.org.uk.

5 Harris, R., *Evaluating Internet Research Sources*, www.virtualsalt.com/evalu8it.htm.

6 Filamentality, www.kn.pacbell.com/wired/fil/.

7 Webquests, http://webquest.sdsu.edu/.

8 *Major Categories in the Taxonomy of Educational Objectives (Bloom 1956)*, http://faculty.washington.edu/krumme/guides/bloom.html.

9 Library and Information Services Council (LISC), *School Libraries: the foundations of the curriculum*, London, HMSO, 1984.

10 The Big 6, www.big6.com/index.php.

11 James Herring's PLUS Model, http://jimmy.qmuc.ac.uk/usr/jherri/plus/default.htm.

12 Department for Education and Employment, Key Stage 3 National Strategy: *Literacy across the Curriculum*. Chapter 6, Reading for information, handout 6.6, p 52, DfEE, 2001.

13 Library Research Service, www.lrs.org/Impact_study.htm.

14 Williams, D., Wavell, C. and Coles, L., *Impact of School Library Services on Achievement and Learning*, Robert Gordon University, 2001, www.resource.gov.uk/documents/impactsl.pdf.

15 Department for Education and Employment, *Key Stage 3 National Strategy: Literacy across the Curriculum*, DfEE, 2001.

16 Department for Education and Skills, *Key Stage 3 Strategy for Foundation Subjects*, DfES, 2003.

17 Smith, A., *Accelerated Learning in Practice: brain based methods for accelerating motivation and achievement*, Network Educational Press, 1998.

18 Smith, A., *Accelerated Learning in the Classroom*, Network Educational Press, 1996.

19 Prashnig, B., *The Power of Diversity*, David Bateman Ltd, 1998.

7

Reader development

CILIP recommends that the school librarian play a lead role in developing a whole-school reading culture, promoting literacy and reading for pleasure.

Reader development describes the pro-active way libraries work to create the best possible reading experiences for everyone.

Their Reading Futures[1]

Reader development is about starting with the reader, opening up new reading horizons, taking reading off the page and into the lives of readers, putting enjoyment at the heart of the reading experience, and making connections between readers. School librarians are uniquely placed to make a significant contribution to the encouragement of reading and the creation of a reading culture across the whole school community.[2]

No single place at school is more important in developing reading than the school library.

Paul Kropp, *The Reading Solution*[3]

Current research into young people's reading habits[4] reinforces the urgent need to identify innovative ways in which the relationship between the reader and the book can be explored, supported and stimulated, especially given the rapidly developing media and technological innovations competing for young people's time and attention.

Developing an awareness of these findings will enable the school librarian to generate appropriate strategies to suit all readers as well as potential readers, regardless of age, gender, background or previous reading experience. Strategies include:

- enthusing individual readers
- supporting specific groups
- being a reading role model
- enlisting the support of colleagues, both teaching and support staff, in raising the reading profile across the curriculum
- getting the whole school reading
- involving the community in reading initiatives
- forming reading partnerships with outside agencies including public libraries.

Many public libraries are doing interesting work to bring reading to young people. One of the major recommendations of the *Start with the Child* report[5] is that school libraries begin to operate collaboratively to create lifelong readers via reading groups, shared resources, staff training, etc.

Reader development not only empowers the reader, it promotes an appreciation of the value of reading and infuses a love of reading for life. It should also shape service delivery, and involve the readers themselves through consultation on the stock, its promotion and use.

Thinking about specific aims will enable the targeting of clearly differentiated client groups in line with the current library development plan and budget.

The school library and the reading curriculum

Reader development and pedagogy are not mutually exclusive or contradictory but rather two sides of the same coin. There is clear evidence that reader development and the active involvement of the school librarian raise educational attainment[6] and that a love of reading is more important in determining academic achievement than social background.[7]

The school librarian should argue that reader development will positively enhance the school's aims and priorities in line with current educational agendas such as:

- national priorities and initiatives
- citizenship
- peer mentoring
- social inclusion and disaffection

- equal opportunities
- lifelong learning
- personal and social development
- consultation with and involvement of students
- community partnerships
- the pastoral context and holistic development
- school self-evaluation processes.

Self-evaluation (see also Chapter 9)

Any process of self-evaluation that is used should tackle fundamental issues in terms of reader development and key questions should be asked:

- How well is the library used in meeting the literacy objectives of the school?
- How is the library promoting reading for pleasure as an activity to be continued beyond the library and beyond school hours?
- Does the library staff encourage students and staff to read widely and confidently?
- Does the library cater for all levels of reading interest and ability?

These key questions are crucial in shaping the library collection, ensuring that the stock contains wide reading opportunities with a good range of genres and formats at different levels that offer both challenge and progression. The stock should validate all reading choices and make all kinds of reading matter, including such formats as magazines, graphic novels and websites. Fiction as well as non-fiction should be actively promoted and integrated where appropriate. It should be well presented and relevant to young people's interests and developmental needs, allowing them to see the world as others see it. Up to date, accessible and attractive, the reading-rich library is well signed and guided with appropriate mechanisms in place to allow reading suggestions and recommendations between peers. These could take the form of reading groups, book chains, buddy schemes, involvement in national reading promotions and challenges or book bulletin boards. Above all, the school librarian should be familiar with the collection and constantly consult with students about their reading needs and choices. The old adage of 'the right book for the right reader at the right time' is never more true than during the secondary school years.

Reading across the curriculum

Reading is no longer the preserve of the English Department. As reading champion, the school librarian should take every opportunity to promote reading in every subject area – taking topic-linked boxes into classrooms, using

The CILIP Guidelines for Secondary School Libraries

fiction in tutorial and guidance lessons, picture books in child development, sci-fi in physics, multicultural fiction in geography, etc.

Brain-based reading

Current educational thinking is firmly focused on how we learn. Reading engages both emotion and intellect – left and right brain hemispheres – and thinking skills are very similar to what we have traditionally taught as 'information-handling skills'. Keeping up to date with, understanding and adapting the latest theories will ensure that librarians are accepted as co-professionals in the educational arena. Useful references include:

- Greenfield's brain research[8]
- Gardner's multiple intelligences[9]
- Goleman's emotional intelligence[10,11]
- Claxton's learning dispositions[12]
- Costa's habits of mind[13]
- Prashnig's learning styles.[14]

Being aware of one's own learning styles and preferences has huge implications for the way we design the ideal reading environment and develop creative reading activities. Research proves that the way we learn determines how we teach. Catering for all kinds of learners – visual, auditory and kinaesthetic – will not only enhance learning but significantly improve behaviour and create more positive attitudes towards books and reading for life.

Reader development and ICT

Young people's engagement with ICT facilitates and motivates literacy rather than displacing reading.

Elaine Millard, *Differently Literate*[15]

Harnessing young people's interest in mobile phones, videos, e-mail, computer gaming and the internet can be a powerful motivator for encouraging the regular reading habit. Enlist the support of colleagues or technically expert students to support activities and include a wider sector of the school community. Successful activities can include:

- txtmsging reviews
- video book ads – staff talking of their favourite reads
- videoconferencing with other school reading groups
- videoconferencing an author visit
- creating snappy book/magazine jingles and trailers

Chapter 7 Reader development **51**

- creating digital photograph displays
- devising a photostory
- developing a reading website.

The internet opens up amazing opportunities for taking reading out of the curriculum and into the lives of young people. It promotes reading not only as an essential skill but also a pleasurable occupation. Young people can be infused with a love of reading for life through participating in online reading discussions, posting reviews, creating bookmarks, playing book-related online games, taking part in virtual reading groups and festivals and e-mailing authors.

Note that content should always be checked before promoting sites, creating bookmarks and using online discussion groups. Policies should be compatible with all other school acceptable use policies and should be drawn up in consultation with your users.

Creating a whole-school reading culture

Reader development is all about promoting reading as a creative rather than passive activity, and opening up books is the most powerful thing that can be done to create a school reading culture among staff and students. Sharing activities can generate a huge interest in reading. Some simple but effective options are listed below:

- Word of mouth recommendations
- Buddy schemes – pairing up students to choose, read and share books together
  - The most common pairings are post-16 students and reluctant younger readers, 11-year-olds with 10-year-olds to ease primary/secondary transition, less able 15-year-olds with 13-year-old students to boost confidence and reading stamina. Experiment to find a solution that meets your school and students' reading needs
- Reading groups – meeting before, during or after school where everyone reads the same book or within the same genre or recommends a personal favourite
  - Groups can be made up of single or mixed year groups, boys or girls only or fans of a particular title, series or author
- Book chains using comment/feedback cards for the next reader to add to
- Displays of students' comments
- Author visits or live reading events
- Poetry performances and storytelling sessions
- Visits by creative artists or residencies, for example jugglers or graphic novelists

- Book debates
- Shadowing schemes that follow national or regional book awards – e.g. Carnegie/Greenaway for outstanding teenage titles/children's illustration, Torchlight (for 8–12s), Blue Peter, Smarties, Guardian or one of the many successful local awards
  - All of these make students' reading opinions matter and emphasize the synergy between books and ICT
- Screen savers across the school network that promote books and library events
- Community volunteer programmes
- 'Top ten' displays
- Leaving books lying where students will pick them up rather than shelving them – on computer tops, chairs or study tables.

Creating a reading calendar using national promotions for specific months or times of year as the basis for reader development activities will ensure something for all sectors of the school community at different times and stages of their school career regardless of previous reading experience or attitude to reading. Keep the profile of reading high all year round through events such as:

- World Book Day
- National Poetry Day
- Swap-a-Book Day
- Annual book awards such as those mentioned above
  - These all run during different months thereby providing opportunities to match particular awards to particular year groups
- Summer Reading Challenges
- Black History Month
- Children in Need
- Valentine's Day, etc.

Many of these have stylish and professionally produced promotional material and freely downloadable resources.

Creating the right reading environment is crucial if librarians are to enthuse young people about reading and entice them to read new things in new ways. Bright, colourful, interactive and frequently changing displays catch the eye and the imagination. Comfortable furniture provides space to become engrossed in a book.

A whole-school reading culture starts small with things like displays around the school, dipboxes in tutor rooms, and reading trolleys in the dining room or common room. Move on to encouraging form tutors to talk about their own reading habits, leading book-related assemblies regularly, running Swap-a-Book days, matching books to staff competitions (ensuring that support staff too are included and starting up staff/student reading groups or electing school 'reading champions'.[16]

To really generate excitement around reading, librarians need to start with the young people themselves. Working in partnership with young people in selecting, displaying and promoting stock, changing displays, creating websites and organizing live reading events is vital to success. Such consultation and involvement carry implications for behaviour in the library, create positive attitudes to reading and fulfil the active citizenship agenda.

Working with reading-related professionals and creative artists such as graphic novelists, video producers, songwriters and rap artists or promoting reading related to leisure interests by creating out-of-school hours clubs (such as chess, Warhammer fantasy gaming, web design, video-editing or model-making) will attract new audiences and inspire students to read in new ways.

Evaluating and demonstrating the value-added impact of reader development is crucial. Keep records of all reader development events and activities – library lesson bookings, overheard comments and anecdotes, increasing issue figures as a result of particular promotions or book events, reading diaries, photos, videos, individual success stories, teacher/parent comments, reader satisfaction surveys – and ensure that they are included in annual reports, school and local newspapers and staff meeting agendas. Keeping the profile of reading high in school and demonstrating enthusiasm and success will make change happen. It will ensure that reader development is sustained and increased to create readers for life in the future.

Useful websites

www.boox.org.uk
www.cool-reads.co.uk
www.readingagency.org.uk
www.booktrust.org.uk
www.rif.org.uk
www.literacytrust.org.uk
www.educationextra.org.uk
www.alite.co.uk
www.edwebproject.org/edref.mi.intro.html
www.gregorc.com

References

1 Their Reading Futures, www.theirreadingfutures.org.uk/def02.cfm, 2002.

2 Department of National Heritage, *Investing in Children: the future of library*

services for children and young people, London, HMSO, 1995.
3 Kropp, P. and Cooling, W., *The Reading Solution: making your child a reader for life*, Penguin, 1995.
4 National Reading Campaign: a National Literacy Trust initiative, Reading Habits, Research and Statistics, www.literacytrust.org.uk/database/Read.html.
5 Chartered Institute of Library and Information Professionals, *Start with the Child: report of the CILIP working group on library provision for children and young people*, CILIP, 2002, www.cilip.org.uk/advocacy/startwiththechild/startwiththechild.pdf.
6 Lance, K. C., *The Impact of School Library Media Centers on Academic Achievement*, ERIC Digest ED372759, www.ericfacility.org/resources.html, 1994
7 OECD, *Reading for Change: performance and engagement across countries*, 2002, www.pisa.oecd.org/Docs/Download/ReadingExeSummary.pdf.
8 Greenfield, S., *The Human Brain: a guided tour*, Phoenix Press, 2000.
9 Gardner, H., *Frames of Mind*, New York, Basic Books, 1985.
10 Goleman, D., *Emotional Intelligence: why it can matter more than IQ*, Bloomsbury, 1996.
11 Goleman, D. *Working with Emotional Intelligence*, Bloomsbury, 1999.
12 Claxton, G., *Building Learning Power: helping young people become better learners*, TLO Ltd, 2000.
13 Costa, A. L., Habits of mind series (5 vols), Association for Supervision and Curriculum Development, 2000.
14 Prashnig, B., *The Power of Diversity*, David Bateman Ltd, 1998.
15 Millard, E., *Differently Literate: boys, girls and the schooling of literacy*, RoutledgeFalmer, 1997.
16 National Reading Campaign: a National Literacy Trust initiative, Campaign activities – Reading Champions, www.literacytrust.org.uk/campaign/champions.html.

8

Marketing, promotion and advocacy

CILIP recommends that the school library be proactively marketed in response to evidence-based analysis of the needs of all potential users.

Marketing is the management process responsible for identifying, anticipating and satisfying customer requirements profitably.
Marketing Definition – Chartered Institute of Marketing[1]

A school librarian must constantly market the school library, to ensure that it is relevant and responsive to the needs of the school community and that it is promoted effectively to appropriate audiences both existing and new.

Marketing activity is frequently associated with promotional activity and advertising. In reality it is a much broader management tool, offering organizations a framework to understand demand, analyse and predict future customer needs and plan, promote appropriate services and provide appropriate resources both to satisfy existing users and to attract new ones.

Marketing theory originated in the commercial sector, but increasingly libraries, in common with other non-profit making and charitable organizations, are recognizing the relevance of marketing strategies,[2] which allow them to respond efficiently to their users' needs and plan services and projects that they can confidently predict are relevant and required. A school library that uses a marketing approach will be able to demonstrate to the school's senior management that the library is both genuinely responsive to the needs of the school community and capable of anticipating and satisfying future need.

Many of the traditional management techniques utilized by school librarians are marketing strategies:

- library management systems offer enormously valuable market analysis data
- promotional activities such as World Book Day and book weeks are important promotional strategies for school libraries' marketing
- consultation with staff and students in preparation for writing a development plan is an exercise in market needs analysis.

The marketing mix for the school library

There are key factors that determine users' perceptions of a service and that can be controlled to manage demand. These are referred to as the 'marketing mix'[3] and are the basic considerations of any marketing strategy. A school library must honestly consider each of these in relation to the needs of students, staff and all potential users to successfully market itself. Successfully marketing a new project requires the same themes to be addressed.

- **Product**
  The range, quality and features of the services the school library offers, including the range of resources and activities such as study support and reading groups. To what extent do these reflect the needs of users and non-users?
- **Price**
  While the school library service may be free at point of access to students and staff, there may be costs associated with its use which determine demand. Fines and charges for lost and damaged items can be a powerful deterrent to use.
- **Promotion**
  Communication with all potential users through use of the school website, intranet, magazines, presentations in assembly or to staff, governors' or management meetings. Different audiences require different styles of communication and different messages.
- **Place/physical distribution**
  Opening times, location of the library sites, including opportunities to virtually access resources or support.
- **People**
  The knowledge, approach and accessibility of all library staff (school librarian and assistants along with student volunteer librarians) are central to the library users' experience of the school library. How friendly and inviting are

Chapter 8 Marketing, promotion and advocacy **57**

the library staff to *all* users?
- **Process**
  Aspects of the school library that enhance the users' experience – guiding, author or subject displays, reading trails – all positively enhance the range and quality of users' experience of the school library.
- **Physical evidence**
  The building and design, layout and furnishings of the library as well as the ambience will determine how attractive it is to potential users.

SWOT analysis

Before developing the marketing plan, it is helpful to reflect on current practice, the strengths and weaknesses, and the opportunities for and threats to development.

This can be done quite easily using a SWOT analysis. The more you can involve service users in this exercise, the better. It is best done with a small group, using a flipchart. Use a brain-storming technique to identify the key strengths, weaknesses, opportunities and threats, and record them as indicated in Figure 8.1.

Writing a marketing plan

Following the SWOT analysis, the marketing plan can be developed. It will set out how a school library service or project will be developed, managed and promoted in response to the needs of potential users. It will be closely linked to, or even be part of, the development plan and will consider the following four core themes:

- needs analysis
- demand forecasting and management
- costing and resource management
- promotion management.

1 Needs analysis

Building up a market profile of the needs of the school community is the first step in writing the school library policy or development plan as well as in writing a marketing plan. Promotion is in itself useless unless the library has based its service on genuine needs. Needs analysis is the basic evidence that the library is addressing the genuine requirements of the school community. It presents an opportunity for the school librarian to engage with the diversity of cultures and personal and social needs present within the school.

58   The CILIP Guidelines for Secondary School Libraries

Strengths	Weaknesses
Good fiction stock Interest in reading amongst students Good environment Student helpers (keen) Some good non-fiction stock (e.g. social care, childcare, history, science) Good display areas Good links with some teachers Popular at lunchtimes (especially if wet!) PCs are filtered and monitored Staff commitment Support from line manager (senior teacher) SLS loans support weak stock areas Effective induction programme	Not enough paperback fiction We never see some students Not enough easy chairs Student helpers (skills, confidence) Some very poor non-fiction stock (geography, maths, English lit. crit.) We never see some teachers Distance from English/Humanities block Not enough people to supervise at lunchtimes PC filtering sometimes a problem No strong link to governors Insufficient money to replace 10% of stock annually Information skills embedded only in some curriculum areas Lack of time to liaise with teachers
Opportunities	**Threats**
Special school status might bring opportunities to bid for money Could invite teachers to help spend bookfund by visiting SLS/supplier Could add one unfiltered PC at the librarian's desk Could survey students re their needs – with a prize draw as an incentive Could review library pages on school intranet – ask student group to produce new design concept Could prepare resource lists on intranet to support key classes Could be in the staffroom before school and at morning break to meet teachers	Special schools status might divert funds away from the library English department keen to purchase own resources as library stock is poor New bursar – will he/she understand our needs? New MLE may not enable link to library catalogue Not sure if ICT staff understand library needs and role New VLE may provide resources targeted to curriculum and may not promote library resources

Figure 8.1 SWOT analysis

Needs analysis draws on a wide range of data:

- Many school libraries conduct regular surveys of student attitudes toward the library (either formal surveys or informal tick sheets/interviews) to try to better meet their needs. The activity of filling in a survey automatically raises the profile of the library in the student's mind. It is essential to publicize the results of these surveys and resulting changes to the library. Having engaged with students' opinions about the development of the library it is important that the library demonstrates that they are valued and acted upon.
- Evidence from meetings, plans for school development or statements from staff about the projected demands that the curriculum and learning strategies will make on the library.
- Quantitative data gathered from the library management system providing information on library use patterns, frequency and key areas of interest, which can be analysed by gender and year groups.
- Comments from staff and student discussion groups.
- Feedback books, comment cards or Post-it notes for responses to library provision or suggestions for stock and services.
- Data from user satisfaction questionnaires.
- Analysis of cultural diversity, including languages spoken within the home, and the range of faiths represented within the school.
- Socio-economic indicators – such as students in receipt of free school meals.
- Data on students with special educational needs or those identified as gifted and talented.
- Access to other academic or commercial research or market models profiling young people's attitudes to reading, learning, books, ICT and information.[4]

2 Demand forecasting and management

It is important to forecast the demand for a library service or project. The needs analysis will have revealed the potential market. However the demand from this market will be determined by other factors listed in the marketing mix: What alternative activities are available in the school at the same time? How accessible and attractive is the library environment? What promotion will be undertaken to encourage use?

The school library must be a place for the whole school community, however the school librarian may want to limit access at particular times and will want to focus support on particular groups at other times (support for revision before exams, or visits from feeder primary school groups to support transition, for instance). A wide range of opening times will normally spread general demand to manageable levels. Determining maximum user numbers with the endorsement of the school's senior management is sometimes necessary, both to

The CILIP Guidelines for Secondary School Libraries

ensure health and safety and to enable students to access a service effectively or benefit from the support of the librarian. Defining and publicizing particular times as being designated for specific user groups (reading group time, sixth form study time, etc.) can also successfully manage demand. Similarly the school librarian may manage demand by varying the library environment – having times when music is played or when silent study is encouraged.

3 Costing and resource management

These details will be listed in the school library's development plan and should include:

- design and production of publicity material
- fees for author visits and other activities involving external resources
- additional copies of books required for reading promotions
- staff time required for organization and implementation.

Guidance on the generation of a development plan and a budget is given in Chapters 2 and 3.

4 Promotion management

Promotion is an important part of marketing and has the definite aim of increasing use. However library promotion often stops short of this aim, by increasing awareness but failing to actually impact on levels of use.

It is helpful to consider another marketing mnemonic: AIDA. This stands for **Awareness**, **Interest**, **Desire** and **Action**. The key use of this is to remind us that action will only happen if the other three have been achieved. First comes **awareness** of a service or opportunity. But we need to encourage an **interest** in this on the part of the customer and then a **desire** to obtain the service or opportunity before **action** will take place. Action simply will not happen without the customer first being aware of, then interested in, and finally desirous of the particular product or service.

In terms of library promotion, this means working at all three stages before an increase in use can be expected. An example might be:

Objective: to increase use of the library for homework after school

Awareness: prepare posters and leaflets advertising the opening hours and facilities available. Ensure that publicity reaches students (e.g. by making announcements in assemblies or through individual tutors).

Interest: make sure the publicity includes something to interest the students – key phrases like 'improve your homework marks' or 'somewhere to relax and

Chapter 8 Marketing, promotion and advocacy **61**

do homework after school' might work. Enlist the help of teachers and advertise special sessions for them to provide help to students. Offer special interest talks and activities (e.g. simple science experiments in the library or workshops on different subjects).

Desire: try to appeal to the students' basic needs. Offer refreshments and a chance to 'chill out' after school. If students see others enjoying coming to the library after school, more of them will want to join in. Take a lead from the retail sector and hold special competitions and events for those who attend.

Action: if all these are successful, action (i.e. students attending) should follow. Once the programme has been implemented, measure the outcomes to see if the objectives were achieved.

Methods of promotion

Variety of promotion is important. Over-exposure to even the best promotion can diminish its impact. Some promotional methods, such as library displays, can be used throughout the school year and become a constant feature of library life. Others, owing to the time and resources needed to run them effectively, may be one-off or annual events only.

It is useful to keep in mind the methods used by bookshops and other retail outlets frequented by young people in promoting their stock. In a bookshop every aspect of space and display is carefully designed to encourage the user to interact with the books. Shelving is not used just to store stock but also to promote it. For example, try monitoring how your users move around the library. Simply changing the position of shelving or altering the method of display to fit with the patterns of your users' movement can be as effective as any big promotional activity. Something as simple as a pile of books left out where students can browse through them can have a significant impact.

In the same way as a business analyses its customer relations, think about the ways in which the library could be made more 'user friendly' to encourage students and staff to come back. How easily can the users find what they need? The following prompts are strategies for addressing promotion to particular target audiences:

Promotion to students

- All new students should be given a basic introduction to the library and to the facilities and services it offers. Build upon this induction at subsequent intervals when the curriculum demands the use of particular facilities or resources. This will have the added benefit of reviving interest periodically in the library. Aim to make the inductions lively and interesting, presenting the library as 'user friendly'.
- Develop an annual plan for the promotion of reading – as described in Chapter 7.

- Demonstrate a willingness to support and value all students in their use of the library via:
  - helpful guiding throughout the library
  - library handbook/guide
  - computerization of the library stock
  - readers' guides (either electronic or paper versions) that help users to define what they need.
- Hold regular book fairs to promote the concept of book ownership. Introduce teachers and students to free bookplates they can download from the internet, or e-mail directly to friends.[5,6]

Promotion to governors and senior management

- Ensure that the library is a regular agenda item.
- Make certain that the library is a positive focus for governors' visits.
- Recommend that a link governor be appointed for the library and be invited to become involved in reading promotions or mentoring schemes.
- Regularly report on the development of the library to governors and senior management and demonstrate the library's commitment to whole-school development issues.

Promotion to teaching staff

There are a number of different avenues for promotion to be explored:

Management
- Ensure that the library development plan implications are addressed at curriculum and other planning meetings.
- Ensure that the integration and use of the library are regular agenda items at staff meetings.
- Attend relevant meetings (departmental, heads of departments, working parties, curriculum development, etc.).

Interpersonal
- Be involved in activities in the school. Informal promotion by library staff while they are attending other school activities can be very effective.

Communication
- Regularly consult with staff, both formally via surveys and informally, to seek their views about the library, its resources and its services.
- Consider appointing a library liaison teacher in each department.
- If there is a newsletter or regular briefing for staff, contribute ideas for library development, opportunities for feedback, details of new books and resources including reviews, information about opening times and services, dates of

Chapter 8 Marketing, promotion and advocacy **63**

mobile library visits, news of special events, etc. – or consider issuing a
dedicated library update newsletter regularly.
* Prepare library information sheets specifically for staff, which highlight all
the available services and facilities. Make sure to update these regularly.
Include information on library resources, websites, online databases,
community resources, etc., which will facilitate staff's teaching.

INSET
* Offer induction sessions for new staff and student teachers, to give them a
tour of the library where resources specific to their curriculum area and
interests can be promoted; also to newly qualified teachers during their
induction course.
* Offer to provide INSET training. INSET days held within the library and
concentrating on library issues can be of enormous benefit in raising the
profile of the library and showing how it can help teachers in the delivery of
the curriculum. The local schools library service should be able to help with
planning and delivering a very effective day or half-day's training, aimed at the
whole staff or selected departments/year groups.

Resources
* Where the schools library service offers a mobile library visit, make sure that
there is staff cover available and that the visit is fully publicized. Maximize
the role of the mobile library in updating staff awareness of resources.
* Discuss with staff the project loan collections available through the schools
library service. Explain how they could be used to support curriculum
delivery, information literacy and reading policies. Give as much help as is
needed to facilitate ordering and planning.
* Provide information services specifically geared to the staff. Services aimed
directly at staff and delivered in a timely, friendly, efficient manner can help
to raise the profile of the library enormously, especially if they save the staff
time and stress. Good practice in selective dissemination of information
shows that it is helpful to maintain a file of individual teachers' specific
interests and requirements.

Promotion to parents and the wider community
* During parent evenings provide opportunities for parents and carers to
browse library resources, including ICT equipment and resources, and to see
examples of work undertaken in the library.
* Offer to hold open days in the library when parents, governors, students and
the larger community can visit and students are on hand to act as guides.
* Offer the library as a focus during curriculum evenings. It may be helpful to
offer to provide sessions on the role of the library in students' learning for

parents and carers.
- Ensure that the parent teacher association (PTA) is fully aware of the role of the library: particularly cost-effective means of offering adequate provision within the library.
- Communicate with parents either via a library newsletter or newspaper or through regular contributions from the library to the school's own newsletter to parents.
- Ensure that the parents are made aware of any mention of the library in the school's inspection report.
- Offer parents the opportunity to work voluntarily within the library. This has the advantage of acquiring extra help for the library as well as raising its profile within the community. Volunteer staff should always be subject to the same rigorous recruitment and disclosure procedures as paid staff within school.
- Involve local media in reporting activities, resources and services.

Advocacy

A school librarian must strive to improve the standards of the school library and the status of the librarian's post in the school.

Rt Hon. Charles Clarke MP, Secretary of State for Education and Skills,
School Libraries Making a Difference[7]

Advocacy is speaking out and winning influence. As education policy tends towards the delegation of management responsibility to each school it is increasingly important for school librarians to act as advocates within their own schools. The first step in any advocacy campaign is to define the target audience and then to tailor the campaign to that audience. Usual targets for a school librarian will be the senior management team, governors, the parents and teachers association or the teaching staff.

Advocacy can assist the school librarian in gaining:

- improved status amongst conflicting and competing priorities
- funding from limited budgets
- new partners who appreciate the library's importance
- recognition of the library's activities as central to the school's mission from head teachers and governors.

Advocacy requires a combination of strategies, with a clear identification of:

- target audience to be influenced – any one of those mentioned above
- identification of advocacy message – determine precisely what the target

Chapter 8 Marketing, promotion and advocacy **65**

audience needs to know, being as concise and economical as possible
- strategy for getting the advocacy message to the target audience – many of the strategies outlined in the section on 'promotion'
- selection of evidence – national and international research is powerful (see online resources detailed below); so too is evidence collected from evaluation of outcomes on learning and teaching in the school (see Chapter 9).

Online advocacy resources

School Libraries Making a Difference. This is a government funded publication and website to support school library advocacy that has been developed by CILIP, SLA and ASCEL (Association of Senior Children's and Education Librarians): www.schoollibrariesadvocacy.org.uk/.

CILIP has produced a range of material to support school librarians' advocacy including a **pack** to help them argue for improved pay and status. This can be downloaded at www.cilip.org.uk/advocacy/empowerment.doc.

Their Reading Futures is a partnership project from the Reading Agency, CILIP, ASCEL and YLG. It aims to take public libraries' work with young readers to a new level. One of the main themes of the project is advocacy and the project website has excellent resources and suggestions for advocacy: www.theirreadingfutures.org.uk/advoc01.cfm.

The Reading Agency has been creating advocacy resources to support librarians. Although these focus on public libraries the strategies and themes are pertinent to school librarians: www.readingagency.org.uk/index2.cfm.

The American Association of School Librarians has compiled an excellent collection of **ready-to-use tools** to conduct an advocacy campaign – large or small – for school libraries: www.ala.org/aasl/advocacy/index.html.

The most comprehensive resource for library advocacy is the American Library Association's *Library Advocates Handbook*. It includes guidance on building an advocacy framework, developing an action plan for promoting the library and communicating with stakeholders: www.ala.org/pio/advocacy/libraryadvocateshandbook.pdf.

The American Library Association's **advocacy resource hub** is at www.ala.org/pio/advocacy/.

References

1 The Chartered Institute of Marketing, www.cim.co.uk/cim/index.cfm.
2 De Sáez, E. E., *Marketing Concepts for Libraries and Information Services*, 2nd edn, Facet Publishing, 2002.
3 Chartered Institute of Library and Information Professionals, *Start with the Child: report of the CILIP working group on library provision for children and young people*, CILIP, 2002,

www.cilip.org.uk/advocacy/startwiththechild/startwiththechild.pdf.

4 ibid.

5 My Home Library, www.myhomelibrary.org/.

6 Bookplates from Anne Fine's website, www.annefine.co.uk/bookplates/.

7 *School Libraries Making a Difference*, a government funded publication developed by CILIP, SLA and ASCEL, 2003, www.schoollibrariesadvocacy.org.uk/.

9

Evaluation

CILIP recommends that the school library evaluate its performance regularly through a programme of self-evaluation agreed with the school's senior management.

Monitoring and evaluation are essential in order to set priorities and decide what action to take to improve the school's quality and raise the achievements of its students.

OFSTED Handbook for Inspecting Secondary Schools[1]

Evaluation is a key part of a school's cycle of planning and development, and the evaluation of the library is an important element in that process. This chapter will examine:

- the management of evaluation and the different types of evidence to be gathered
- the difference between inputs, outputs and outcomes
- the main approaches to evaluation
- using the results of evaluation
- the benefits of evaluation.

Evaluation provides valuable information to senior management so that the library, its action plans and targets may take their rightful place in the school's overall agenda. Evaluation will help determine the library's development plans and the professional development agenda of the librarian. It also provides powerful advocacy material when making a case for greater resources, whether they be materials, staffing or accommodation. Evaluation provides valuable information to enable the library to prepare to meet the challenge of future trends and developments, and to do so in the most cost-effective way.

To summarize, effective management is impossible without effective evaluation. It is the way in which the school librarian can learn what impact the library is having on the school, and how it contributes to the development of students – both in terms of their reading development, and in their use of the library to support the curriculum.

A growing emphasis on self-evaluation, with which schools are familiar in other contexts, is a trend that the library should now welcome. Library self-evaluation provides a timely opportunity to be part of the wider agenda and to claim a central and vital role in the life of the school.

Managing evaluation

Evaluating the library requires progress to be measured and evaluated against agreed priorities and objectives using a variety of techniques. These involve monitoring, collecting data to measure performance, evaluating performance through performance indicators, reporting on progress and reviewing targets and objectives.

- **Monitoring** is the ongoing process of collecting and analysing data to enable evaluation to take place. Data should include quantitative data (i.e. numeric measures) and qualitative data (i.e. descriptive evidence of what is happening). One of the main ways of gathering this data should be from the students themselves via consultations, interviews, surveys and observations.
- **Performance measures** are simple measures of 'what is' or 'what has happened' (for example, the number of students in the school, the number of students who are library members, the total number of book issues, or the total number of fiction book issues). They are useful for building performance indicators (see below).
- **Performance indicators** enable the performance of the library to be evaluated through comparisons. Comparisons can be made with the library's past performance (e.g. last term, last year), or with other comparable libraries or services (e.g. other school libraries). They can be quantitative (numeric) or qualitative (descriptive).
  - *Quantitative performance indicators* are created by combining the data from at least two performance measures, to give useful indicators of the levels of actual performance (e.g. the percentage of students who are library

members; the percentage of the issues that are fiction books). The school librarian's challenge is to select the most appropriate indicators to use to reflect progress towards the library's main objectives or targets.

— *Qualitative performance indicators* describe a target level of achievement. For example, 'The library is perceived by senior managers to be at the heart of the school' or 'The library encourages reading for pleasure and develops individual students in their reading confidence'. Objective evidence for these indicators can be more difficult to obtain. The evidence might come from staff and student surveys or interviews, the degree of attention the library gets in key school documents, or from observations and evidence from parents or governors.

• **Reporting on progress**
The results of evaluation should be used to report to others on the role the library plays in the school. Regular appropriate reporting will alert others to the work of the library, and the contribution it makes to learning and teaching. This can be done in an annual report or through special reports or bids for funding.

• **Reviewing targets and objectives**
Once a year, the library's key objectives and targets should be reviewed as part of the development planning process. At the same time, performance measures and indicators should be reviewed. New performance indicators will need to be developed for any new priority areas, and can be used in the development plan to show how progress towards the targets will be measured.

Inputs, outputs and outcomes

To collect and analyse data on the full range of library services and resources will require a variety of measures of inputs, outputs and, most powerfully, outcomes.

Inputs

Inputs are traditionally the type of evaluation data most frequently used by librarians. They describe the resources, investment and time that go into the library service. These inputs can be considered against benchmarks (e.g. measures of what the best school libraries are achieving) or against recommendations (e.g. from CILIP, DfES, HMI or the SLA). Schools library services can advise about local, national or regional benchmarks.

The input *measures* that should be monitored and recorded include:

• whether the library has a clear, up-to-date library policy
• how the library policy fits into the aims of the school
• what space the library occupies against recommended levels (see Chapter 4)
• whether the library is staffed by an appropriately qualified librarian with head of department status

The CILIP Guidelines for Secondary School Libraries

- the total annual stock budget
- whether the range of stock reflects all National Curriculum and Literacy requirements, and all age and ability levels
- the library's opening hours and the extent to which they allow access to both class groups and all individual users.

Input *performance indicators* will include:

- the total/average per student expenditure on the library and resources compared to recommended levels (see Chapter 5)
- the percentage of the stock and resources that fully reflect issues of diversity and special needs and are genuinely inclusive
- the level of good quality stock per student against the recommended levels of 13 per student for 11–16 schools and 17 for 16–18 schools.

Input data is usually the easiest to capture and analyse. However, it is frequently the weakest in terms of proving the value of the library. It neither describes what use is made of the library service, nor what the impact is on students, teachers and the wider community. It is important therefore that it is combined with and used alongside measures of outputs and, most significantly, of outcomes.

Outputs

Outputs describe the level and frequency of activity. They can be calculated through the use of electronic gate counts or computer management systems. They can be evaluated against targets (for instance, an increase of $x\%$ in items loaned annually), or against benchmarks (e.g. the output levels that the best school libraries are achieving).

Output *measures* that should be monitored include:

- the number of items loaned
- the number of enquiries
- the number of class visits to the library
- the number of individual library users
- the number of literacy-related activities in the library
- the number of and attendance at other reading development activities, reading promotions, etc.
- the frequency of and attendance at out-of-school-hours activities
- the number of students undertaking programmes of library skills induction and development in each separate year group
- the number of students displaying competence at using the skills they have been taught.

Output *performance indicators* might include:

- the percentage of membership (staff and students) using the library/borrowing items
- the percentage of classes making systematic use of the library
- the percentage of students attending out-of-school-hours activities
- the percentage of students who display competence in using the library skills they have been taught.

Specific outputs can also be used to learn the extent to which the library is engaging with particular target groups:

- loans by year groups
- loans by gender
- use of the library by particular departments.

Outputs alone have a limited power as evaluation data, as they do not indicate whether the activity is actually achieving any impact on users. At best, outputs can demonstrate levels of activity, and user awareness, activity and satisfaction.

Outcomes or impacts

Outcomes or impacts describe the *effect* of the service's inputs and outputs. They can be used to show how people develop, learn and change as a result of the services of the school library and the school librarian. They can show the difference that the school librarian and the library make to individuals, groups and the whole school community. Outcomes are the most powerful evaluation data that the school librarian can use. However, they can be the hardest to measure.

Outcomes can encompass a whole range of behavioural changes. They might demonstrate that students are more motivated and engaged, or that they are reading in new and exciting ways. They might demonstrate that teachers are using new resource-based teaching strategies as a result of the school library. They might describe the way students behave as independent learners in the library or learning resource centre, both in lesson times and outside them, providing evidence of changes in attitude, motivation or level of study skills. The common theme is that they enable the library to demonstrate its impact on people.

Outcomes are best gathered through qualitative (i.e. descriptive) data. To evaluate an outcome it is necessary to go through three stages:

1 Select an appropriate outcome that reflects a school priority or a particular

72 The CILIP Guidelines for Secondary School Libraries

chosen focus (e.g. 'more children will enjoy reading for pleasure').

2 Consider what the success criteria are for that outcome – i.e. which signs will tell you that the outcome is occurring and a positive impact is taking place (e.g. more children will express enjoyment in discussing their reading; teachers will report more children enjoying reading for pleasure).

3 Decide how you can collect the evidence to show that this is happening (e.g. How many children borrow books for pleasure and express enjoyment about them? What do teachers say?).

Outcome evidence that can be collected includes:

- examples of students' talking or writing about what they have enjoyed or learnt through the library
- examples from teachers and parents, showing how their students' learning has been supported by the library
- observation of students' behaviour in the library relating to library intervention; this might include a wider reading range or improved information retrieval skills.

A variety of projects have recently developed frameworks to help librarians to measure outcomes of their services (notably the Reading Agency's 'Their Reading Futures'[2] and Resource's 'Inspiring Learning for All'[3] projects). Both of these offer practical frameworks for evaluating outcomes or impacts and could be used to gather evidence in the school context.

Consultation with students and staff

Consultation is a key way of collecting evidence for evaluation. Evidence drawn from the users of the library, and from the non-users, will be key to evaluating the extent to which the library impacts upon the school. The question 'How can students and teachers help to provide the evidence?' should be asked and answered in every evaluation exercise.

Approaches to evaluation

There are three main approaches to evaluation. These are self-evaluation, peer review and external evaluation.

Self-evaluation

Self-evaluation is the term used to describe the process in which the service is assessed against objectives by its own internal management. It demands a rigorous, open, honest and objective method for assessing the value and effectiveness of the service involved, which all good managers will recognize and welcome. It has the advantage of being an in-house process, the control of which lies with the manager directly responsible for the service. Additionally, with self-evaluation it is unlikely that an important factor will be missed through lack of inside knowledge.

Increasingly, self-evaluation is being recognized as a key strategy for improving standards in schools and other learning institutions. Inspection agencies are actively encouraging, and in some cases, requiring, self-evaluation. School libraries are responding to this development: school libraries in Scotland have a highly developed model for self-evaluation,[4] and the Department for Education and Skills is developing a model for school libraries in England (see the report published by Resource[5]), which was was piloted in 2003 by Information Management Associates, has been revised and will be published in 2004. It will be a major contribution to qualitative evidence-gathering in the school library sector and should be seriously considered by all librarians and senior management teams in schools.

To be effective, self-evaluation needs to be as objective as possible and maintain a clear focus on outcomes rather than on processes. It requires a basic project plan and a specific timescale. The findings and conclusions from self-evaluation should be used as a basis of revising the school library development plan.

In planning self-evaluation the following key points need to be considered:

- **Which area of the service to evaluate**
  It is unlikely that self-evaluation will examine all areas of the library service. It is much more likely that a specific area will be addressed initially and over a period of time the self-evaluation process can gradually cover all key areas of the library service.

  The focus of the self-evaluation needs to be selected by the school librarian in discussion with the senior management of the school.
- **Support for self-evaluation**
  Winning the support of the school's senior management for self-evaluation is key for winning support for any resulting action plans. An external 'critical friend' is also advisable, to provide an objective perspective during the self-evaluation process. This role can be undertaken either by a senior professional library colleague from another school or ideally by a member of the local schools library service.
- **What data to collect and how to collect it**
  Once the main focus is agreed, there is a need to identify how evidence will be collected. This may be quantitative data (e.g. the number of students observed displaying certain behaviours) or qualitative data (e.g. observations

74 The CILIP Guidelines for Secondary School Libraries

of behaviours, and/or interviews to determine students' and teachers' opinions and views about the value of the library).

- **Drawing conclusions and sharing them**
  The evidence will need collating, and then analysing for key messages about the impact the library is having. The librarian will need to produce a summary of findings, and draw some conclusions and recommendations in the light of what has been learned. For example, if the impact study shows that in relation to independent learning the library is felt to have a significant impact on student skills for a particular year group, it may be appropriate to recommend extending the information-skills programme to other years.

  The findings will be a powerful lever to support library development. They need also to be presented to the wider school community, especially to the senior management team and to governors.

Peer review

Peer review is a valuable form of evaluation, which combines the rigour of external inspection with the informed view of the specialist. Peer review takes place where one or more professionals with a similar background and experience (i.e. peers), but who work in an external context (e.g. other schools in the same authority, or schools from another authority) provide external evaluation combined with ideas and support. It can be a reciprocal arrangement, where staff from different schools can agree to review one another's performance.

Peer review can be useful for comparing outputs and for evaluating outcomes. It can provide an informed but external view that is at the same time rigorous and supportive. It can be used to compare data, or can also be applied to process management. In this case it would be used to evaluate how things are done and whether there are alternative ways of achieving the same or improved outcomes.

To discuss the possibilities of peer review, the school librarian's first port of call should be the local schools library service. The results of peer review can be used in exactly the same way as those from self-evaluation.

External evaluation

Schools are systematically appraised by statutory inspection and it would be natural to expect the inspection bodies to evaluate the school library and highlight its impact on learning and teaching. However, in practice, many inspections fail to engage rigorously with the school library. Recent moves have sought to remedy this: in 2000 Ofsted published guidance notes on the inspection of school libraries[6] and similar improvements have emerged in the Welsh and Scottish inspection agencies.

In order to gain the most benefit from any inspection, it is essential that the school librarian should prepare thoroughly. Many schools library services will

Chapter 9 Evaluation **75**

offer pre-inspection support. Preparation should include:

- Presentation of evidence of self-evaluation of the school library to the school's senior management in advance of the inspection to be forwarded to the inspection team.
- Preparation of a portfolio of activities and evidence of outcomes on teaching, learning, reading and motivation, which can be presented to inspectors during inspection visits to the library. Remember to include evidence of out-of-school-hours activities. Evidence of self-evaluation should also be included. Evidence should include differentiated examples of students' work (three ability levels in each case).
- A summary of quantitative data showing the level of basic library activity in terms of inputs and outputs.

Evidence should be prepared and gathered in an accessible format ready to share with the external inspectors. It is always advisable to assume that the inspectors will have little pre-knowledge of the school library – so it is important not to omit information that may seem obvious to the school librarian.

The value of external inspection is that the school library is measured alongside all other aspects of the school. Where the inspection identifies the value of the library to the quality of teaching and learning, this can be a powerful support for future school library development. Where the inspection identifies weaknesses in the school library, this can be a valuable support in gaining the required resources for any developments (e.g. new location, improved space, adequate staffing) that may be needed.

Using the results of evaluation

Evaluation is not a standalone activity, but needs to be linked into a cycle of continuous improvement and development. The aim of evaluation is to improve the library in the light of what is discovered. The results should be used to inform the librarian's plans, policies and practice. They should be shared widely within the school to enable library development to be closely linked to whole-school developments. Difficult messages from the evidence should not be ignored, but need to be confronted and reported to management as appropriate. The findings can be used in a variety of ways:

- new priorities and plans may be identified for the development plan
- results can be highlighted in reports to senior managers or the governing body, with requests for funding for projects to address areas of need that have emerged
- results can be used as evidence in budget bids

- new services may be planned, to meet newly identified needs
- budget planning may be adjusted to reflect changing priorities or areas of particular need that have emerged from the findings
- the arrangement of stock may be changed to improve accessibility
- new promotions may be arranged to develop awareness of some services or resources
- new ideas may be piloted to achieve specific aims (e.g. a new style of induction, or new ways of working with subject teachers)
- simple day-to-day changes might be made in the way the library operates for students and teachers
- the results of evaluation, and especially any changes in policy and practice that are made as a result, should be documented and used as evidence of good practice in the portfolio presented to external inspectors.

The benefits of evaluation

Evaluation should be used to track progress towards the library's key aims. It should be used to show progress against the key areas of the library policy and the development plan. It should also, most importantly, include the ways in which students are using and benefiting from library resources and services – in other words, what the library is achieving for the school community. A key question for school library managers should be 'to what extent is the library an asset to the school, and can it demonstrate through its resources and its use that it makes a difference to learning and teaching?' This is what the effective school librarian will want to know anyway, in order to plan for continuous improvement of the library and its services. Evaluation skills are therefore central to a good manager's portfolio of skills.

References

1　Office for Standards in Education (Ofsted), *Handbook for Inspecting Secondary Schools, with Guidance on Self-evaluation*, The Stationery Office, 1999.

2　Their Reading Futures, www.theirreadingfutures.org.uk.

3　Inspiring Learning for All, www.resource.gov.uk/action/learnacc/00insplearn.asp.

4　SLIC, *Taking a Closer Look at the School Library Resource Centre*, SLIC, 1999, www.slainte.org.uk/Slicpubs/schoolpis.pdf.

5　McNicol, S. and Elkin, J., *School Libraries: the design of a model for self-evaluation*, Cirt: The Centre for Information Research, 2003, www.resource.gov.uk/documents/id356rep.doc.

6　Office for Standards in Education, *Appendix D: Inspecting School Libraries and Learning Resource Centres*, www.ofsted.gov.uk/publications/docs/update36/update36-08.htm.

10
Partnerships

> **CILIP recommends that the school librarian work in partnership with key internal and external partners to improve the quality of the school library.**

The school library sits at the heart of a network of partnerships. As well as the vital partnerships within the school with teaching departments, governors, senior management and student forums there must also be an external network of partnerships. These make the school library relevant to the wider learning community, adding new dimensions to provision and informing development and marketing.[1]

Schools library services (SLSs)

The most fundamental partnership for every school library is with its schools library service. An unpublished report by HMI in the 1980s showed that for every £1 spent with a schools library service, schools were likely to benefit with resources to the value of £9. This makes the option of hiring resources from an SLS a very economic prospect.

SLSs are the central library support services that operate in 85% of UK local authorities and that support school librarians, libraries and teachers. Currently 71% of school children in the UK benefit from the support offered by an SLS.[2] In authorities where SLSs do not exist, neighbouring authorities will frequently offer services.

SLSs have a powerful contribution to play in enabling schools to realize their aims. Their information management expertise and awareness of government priorities and policies relating to literacy and learning can be a powerful force in supporting schools in delivering national strategies. Many SLSs have had key roles in the delivery of the Key Stage 3 strategy in English schools.[3] Others have delivered important programmes for improving learning resource provision across an authority to help deliver key local education authority targets.[4]

While SLSs exist in most authorities in the UK, national legislation means that they function in differing ways. In Northern Ireland they are a statutory service. In England, following a period during the 1990s when the Local Management of Schools encouraged many local education authorities (LEAs) to delegate their funding, the introduction of Fair Funding Regulations has required all SLSs to delegate their funding for secondary schools. For some SLSs delegation of budgets has resulted in cuts and/or contraction of services and, in a few cases, closure. Others have benefited from the freedoms that their new trading status has offered, and some are now generating more income from project activities than they are from schools buying back their core service provision. SLSs remain key partners for school libraries who seek to improve the quality, effectiveness and range of their services.

SLS services

Each SLS will provide full details of the support and services offered, and where applicable the cost of this support. The services offered to schools will either be in the form of a pick-and-choose menu or a pre-defined package of services – or a mixture of both. These will generally include the following elements:

- learning resource provision
- consultancy
- support for evaluation
- training
- partnership development.

Learning resource provision

Many SLSs lend large numbers of resources in a wide variety of formats to schools. These resources are chosen to meet the needs of the curriculum and suit the ability of particular groups. SLS staff also assist schools to purchase resources (through book talks, bibliographies, electronic resources, exhibition collections and bookshop services). Some SLSs offer 'shelf-ready' stock, complete with classification and cataloguing and ready-to-use jacketing and other stationery.

Consultancy

- SLSs have wide experience in designing, planning and equipping school libraries. The SLS will know of examples of good practice in the local education authority and in the region
- Many SLSs offer advice and support in the recruitment of school library staff.

Support for evaluation

- **Preparation and response to inspection**
  SLS staff can provide advice pre- and post-inspection. They can support action plans, particularly in areas such as improving the standards of the school library and in information skills provision.
- **Support for self-evaluation**
  SLS staff can act as a 'critical friend', supporting the school librarian in self-evaluating, and can advise on or even organize opportunities for peer review.
- **Benchmarking**
  Many SLSs collate data relating to school library provision to enable schools to benchmark themselves against local, regional or national levels and trends.

Training

Most SLSs offer INSET for teachers and librarians from individual schools or groups of schools. Many SLSs played an active role in delivering the New Opportunities Funded ICT training for school librarians and have continued to develop their support for CPD.

Partnership development

The SLS is the focal point for school librarians within the LEA, facilitating networking and professional meetings where knowledge, experience and good practice can be shared amongst school librarians. The SLS can act as an important bridging agency linking the school library into the local public library service. SLSs are also closely linked to the local education authority, and provide the school librarian with invaluable contacts in the wider education structures.

Making best use of the SLS

The individual school will decide the nature and level of support to be requested from the SLS. One key decision is the balance to be made between resources that are purchased directly, and those borrowed or leased from the SLS. The decision should be informed by the considerations listed below.

Purchasing resources is the most appropriate decision for:

- items that are needed constantly (e.g. frequently used reference resources)

- items that are used regularly to support teaching
- items that are likely to be in constant or regular demand
- items that are needed to form the core stock of the school library.

Hiring or leasing resources may be more appropriate for:

- items that are used only occasionally
- new items that the librarian wants to trial before purchase
- items where the library will benefit from a regular change-over of stock (e.g. fiction)
- items needed for a short-term purpose (e.g. an exhibition, or display on a particular topic, or a topic being studied by a group of students for a particular time period, or the need for extra books on a topic where there is considerable demand at one time).

Other key partners

As schools are increasingly seen within the context of the wider education community ... the need for the school library to be at the hub of a network of learning partnerships is more important than ever before.

Start with the Child[5]

In addition to working with the SLS, the school librarian will develop and manage a range of partners. These will be determined by the school's aims as reflected in the library development plan. Key partners will frequently include:

- parents
- feeder schools
- further and higher learning institutions
- public libraries
- youth service, careers service, Connexions[6]
- the book trade.

Parents

Partnership with parents is essential for the proper support of students. This can be achieved through home–school liaison schemes, through the PTA, or through special library-focused projects. Some examples where parent partnerships can be beneficial are listed below.

- PTA support for capital projects and items of library expenditure beyond the basic budgets (e.g. special furniture or equipment which will enhance the library environment).

Chapter 10 Partnerships   **81**

- Home–school liaison schemes can facilitate communication and support family learning. The librarian can support by involving use of the library in such projects, supporting student learning and library use and helping parents learn how regular library use can help their children. Such schemes are invaluable in providing a communication channel to parents, and the school librarian should provide inspiring articles about reading, libraries and learning for any publications produced for parents through such schemes. Family learning schemes also offer an obvious role for the school library, particularly when students reach GCSE stage and parents need to know more about how library servies can support investigative learning styles.
- Special projects might include library exhibitions or author visits, lads and dads projects, special events or regular out-of-school clubs or homework sessions. Parents can assist by attending as volunteers to support library activities when large audiences of students are involved. They may help by providing refreshments, or by acting as guides or 'meeters and greeters' for special events. They are valuable sources of additional administrative help for the library, which can sometimes be a helpful and supportive environment for work experience for those who are contempating a return to the workplace. Parents can also provide a valuable source of volunteer helpers for out-of-school homework or reading clubs. Many parents also can offer sessions sharing a skill or hobby, to contribute to a book week or club programme.

It is important to keep parents informed of school library developments, as well as telling the students. It is useful to provide a handout or publicity card, which students can take home to show parents (e.g. a flyer about a new homework club, or a message about using the public library over the summer holiday) in order to get key messages across. Alternatively, the school website is an obvious (and cheap) alternative as a means of communicating with parents.

Feeder schools

Collaboration between primary and secondary librarians is important in order to support the transition between primary and secondary education. Secondary students can act as reading mentors in primary schools, and stock and information, displays, etc. can be co-ordinated and shared. Another valuable link can be made through visits by arranging for primary students to visit the secondary school library. This enables them to see the library services available to them, and learn how the new school library is actually a manageable development from that in their primary school.

Further and higher learning institutions

Vocational learning and new ways of delivering 14–19 learning are necessitating much closer links between secondary and FE institutions. Initiatives include access to one another's catalogues and collections, joint staff training and co-ordinated approaches to developing information literacy.

Neighbouring secondary schools

Building partnerships with neighbouring secondary schools can be extremely beneficial. Library catalogues can be combined electronically to facilitate inter-library loan and librarians can meet to share expertise and plan joint events. Funding for specific areas of resource development may be shared and the costs for special events such as author visits can be borne jointly. Students can also benefit from interaction through activities such as book fairs and Carnegie shadowing.

Public libraries

Co-ordination of reader-development and study-support initiatives between the school library and local public library is useful to avoid expensive and unnecessary duplication. The school library can be valuable in promoting summer reading initiatives. The public library meanwhile has a key role to play in supporting the school library in promoting family literacy, providing access to a wide range of imaginative literature, and supporting the day-to-day information needs of individual children and young people. It is therefore helpful if the school librarian can keep the local library informed of areas of likely demand.

Youth service, careers service, Connexions[5]

The school library is an invaluable location for providing personal and social information for members of the school community. It is also a unique and neutral location which can provide a base for adviser/student interaction, and resources to support individual and personal development and career choices.

The book trade

Local booksellers and publishers can provide useful support in planning a reading promotion, booking an author or providing posters and promotional materials.

Making partnerships work

Partnerships need to be managed if they are to work effectively. This requires excellent communication, clear project planning and a willingness to adapt while retaining a clear sense of one's own priorities.

Successful management of partnerships requires:

Chapter 10 Partnerships **83**

- selection of relevant and proven partners
- definition of common ground, exploration of realistic mutual benefits and definition of the purpose of the partnership
- the establishing of mechanisms ensuring effective communication
- monitoring of the partnership
- evaluation of the partnership, with formal structures for thanking partners and feeding back the outcomes of a project to all partners.

As well as being an essential fact of life, partnerships can be enjoyable experiences – broadening partners' experience, enabling them to discover more about varied institutions and agencies, and providing allies who can assist the library to achieve its objectives.

Notes and references

1 Library and Information Commission, *Empowering the Learning Community: report of the Education and Libraries Task Group to the Secretaries of State for Culture, Media & Sport and for Education & Employment*, HMSO, 2002.

2 Creaser, C. and Maynard, S., *A Survey of Library Services to Schools and Children in the UK 2001–2002*, Library and Information Statistics Unit, 2002.

3 For instance Birmingham SLS's *Talking Texts* project, www.birmingham.gov.uk/slsadvice.bcc

4 Coventry Education Library Service, *Review of Post-16 Resources and Facilities in Coventry Schools*, Coventry City Council, 2002.

5 Chartered Institute of Library and Information Professionals, *Start with the Child: report of the CILIP working group on library provision for children and young people, CILIP*, 2002, www.cilip.org.uk/advocacy/startwiththechild/startwiththechild.pdf.

6 Connexions is an information and advice service for young people. It covers personal issues such as health and money as well as information on career and learning options. More information is available on www.connexions-direct.com.

Bibliography and further reading

Abbott, J., *The Child is Father of the Man*, 21st learning initiative, 1999, www.21learn.org.

Ball, F., *Supporting Special Educational Needs in the Secondary School LRC: SLA guideline*, SLA, 2002.

Barnett, D. and Dubber, G., *Balancing the Books: managing the secondary school LRC budget: SLA guideline*, SLA, 2002.

Berger, P. *Internet for Active Learners: curriculum-based strategies for K-12*, American Library Association, 1998.

Birmingham Schools Library Service, *The Difference We're Making*, Birmingham Advisory and Support Service, 2002.

Chambers, A., *Introducing Books to Children*, 2nd edn, Heinemann, 1983.

Charlton, L., *Planning and Designing a Secondary School Library Research Centre*, SLA, 2002.

Chartered Institute of Library and Information Professionals, *The Primary School Library Guidelines*, CILIP, 2002.

Chartered Institute of Library and Information Professionals, *Report of the National Information Policy - Policy Action Group*, 2002, www.cilip.org.uk.

Chartered Institute of Library and Information Professionals, *Start with the*

Child: report of the CILIP working group on library provision for children and young people, CILIP, 2002, www.cilip.org.uk/advocacy/startwiththechild/startwiththechild.pdf.

Chartered Institute of Library and Information Professionals, *School Libraries Making a Difference*, CILIP, 2003.

Claxton, G., *Building Learning Power: helping young people become better learners*, TLO Ltd, 2000.

Cooling, W. (comp.), *Books to Enjoy: with boys in mind*, SLA, 1999.

Cooling, W. (comp.), *More Books to Enjoy: 12-16*, SLA, 2000.

Cornish, G., *Keep it Legal: copyright guidance for school library staff, SLA guideline*, SLA, 2003.

Costa, A. L., Habits of mind series (5 vols.), Association for Supervision and Curriculum Development, 2000.

Coventry Education Library Service, *Review of Post-16 Resources and Facilities in Coventry Schools*, Coventry City Council, 2002.

Creaser, C. and Maynard, S., *A Survey of Library Services to Schools and Children in the UK 2001-2002*, Library and Information Statistics Unit, 2002.

Department for Education and Employment, *Empowering the Learning Community*, HMSO, 2000.

Department for Education and Employment, *Key Stage 3 National Strategy: Framework for Teaching English: Years 7, 8, and 9*, DfEE 0019/2001.

Department for Education and Employment, *Key Stage 3 National Strategy: Literacy across the Curriculum*, Chapter 6, Reading for information , handout 6.6, DfEE, 2001 .

Department for Education and Skills, *A New Specialist System: transforming secondary education*, DfES, 2003.

Department for Education and Skills, *Area Guidelines for Schools*, www.teachernet.gov.uk/sbareaguidelines, 2003.

Department for Education and Skills, *Key Stage 3 Strategy for Foundation Subjects*, DfES, 2003.

Department of National Heritage, *Schools Library Services and Financial Delegation to Schools*, HMSO, 1994.

Department for National Heritage, *Investing in Children: the future of library services for children and young people*, HMSO, 1995.

Department of National Heritage, *Investing in Children: the future of library services for children and young people*, HMSO, 1996.

de Sáez, E. E., *Promoting the School Library: SLA guideline*, SLA, 2000.

de Sáez, E. E., *Marketing Concepts for Libraries and Information Services*, 2nd edn, Facet Publishing, 2002.

Dewe, M., *Planning and Designing Libraries for Children and Young People*, Library Association Publishing, 1995.

Drury, C. and Dubber, G., *Managing Behaviour in the Secondary School Library: SLA guideline*, SLA, 2001.

Dubber, G., *Teaching Information Skills: SLA guideline*, SLA, 1995.

Dubber, G., *Organising Voluntary Help in the School Library: SLA guideline*, SLA, 1996.

Dubber, G. (ed.), *The Internet, the Secondary School Library and the Independent Learner*, The Library Association, 1999.

Dubber, G., *Library Induction: introducing students and staff to the secondary school library: SLA guideline*, SLA, 2001.

Dubber, G. and Scott, E., *Running a Successful School Library Book Event: SLA guideline*, SLA, 2000.

Elkin, J., *Focus on the Child: libraries, literacy and learning*, Library Association Publishing, 1996.

Ennis, K., (ed.), *Guidelines for Resource Services in Further and Higher Education*, Library Association Publishing, 2000.

Gardner, H., *Frames of Mind: theory of multiple intelligences*, New York, Basic Books, 1985.

Goleman, D., *Emotional Intelligence: why it can matter more than IQ*, Bloomsbury, 1996.

Goleman, D., *Working with Emotional Intelligence*, Bloomsbury, 1999.

Grassian, E. S. and Kaplowitz, J. R., *Information Literacy Instruction: theory and practice*, Neal-Schuman, 2001.

Green, D., *Moving Up: the library resource centre 16–19: SLA guideline,* SLA, 1999.

Greenfield, S., *The Human Brain: a guided tour*, Phoenix Press, 2000.

Further Education Funding Council, *Guidance on Floorspace Management in Further Education Colleges: supplement to circular 97/37*, FEFC, 1997, http://lsc.wwt.co.uk/documents/circulars/fefc_pubs/9737s.pdf.

Hannesdottir, S. K., *Guidelines for the Education and Training of School Librarians*, IFLA, 1986.

Herring, J., *Teaching Information Skills in School*, Library Association Publishing, 1996.

Howard, J., *Information Skills and the Secondary Curriculum: some practical approaches*, British Library, 1991.

IFLA/UNESCO, *The School Library Manifesto*, IFLA, 2000, www.ifla.org/VII/s11/pubs/manifest.htm.

Kinnell, M., *Managing Library Resources in Schools*, Library Association Publishing,1994.

Kropp, P. and Cooling, W., *The Reading Solution: making your child a reader for life*, Penguin, 1995.

Lemaire, K., *Shelf Life, Shelf Matters: managing resources in the school library:*

SLA guideline, SLA, 2001.

Library and Information Commission, *Empowering the Learning Community: report of the Education and Libraries Task Group to the Secretaries of State for Culture, Media & Sport and for Education & Employment*, HMSO, 2002.

Library and Information Services Council (LISC), *School Libraries: the foundations of the curriculum*, HMSO, 1984.

Lighthall, L. and Haycock, K., *Information Rich but Knowledge Poor? emerging issues for schools and libraries worldwide*, IASL, 1997.

Malone, G. and Smith, D., *Learning to Learn: developing study skills with children who have special educational needs*, NASEN, 1996.

Marland, M., *Information Skills in the Secondary Curriculum*, Methuen, 1981.

Martin, R. and Rader, H., *Information and IT Literacy: enabling learning in the 21st century*, Facet Publishing, 2003.

McKenzie, J. *Beyond Technology: questioning, research and the information literate school*, FNO Press, 2000.

McNicol, S., Nankivell, C. and Elkin, J., *Children, Access and Learning: resource based learning and the impacts of environment and learning cultures*, University of Central England, 2002.

Millard, E., *Differently Literate: boys, girls and the schooling of literacy*, RoutledgeFalmer, 1997.

Morris Hargreaves McIntyre, *Start with the Child: the needs and motivations of young people. A report commissioned by Resource and CILIP*, 2002, www.resource.gov.uk/documents/re179rep.pdf.

Murphy, R., *Going Online: developing LRC web pages: SLA guideline*, SLA, 2003.

National Youth Agency, *Hear by Right*, NYA, 2003, www.4youthinc.co.uk/hear.htm.

OECD, *Reading for Change: performance and engagement across countries*, 2002, www.pisa.oecd.org/Docs/Download/ReadingExeSummary.pdf.

Office for Standards in Education, *Handbook for Inspecting Schools*, Ofsted, 2002.

Office for Standards in Education, *Handbook for Inspecting Secondary Schools: for inspections from September 2003*, Ofsted, 2003.

Office of Arts and Libraries, *School Libraries: the foundations of the curriculum*, HMSO, 1986.

Prashnig, B., *The Power of Diversity*, David Bateman Ltd, 1998.

Resource, *Disability Portfolio*, Resource, 2003.

Resource, *Inspiring Learning for All: a vision for accessible learning in museums, archives and libraries*, www.resource.gov.uk/action/learnacc/00insplearn.asp.

Rogers, R. (ed.), *Teaching Information Skills: a review of research and its impact on education*, Bowker Saur, 1994.

Scott, E., *Managing the Internet in the Primary and Secondary School Library:*

SLA guideline, SLA, 2000.

Scott, E., *Measuring Success: how effective is your school library resource centre: SLA guideline*, SLA, 2001.

Sheffield Hallam University, *Survey of Secondary School Libraries: a report prepared for CILIP*, October, 2002, www.cilip.org.uk/practice/ssl.html.

SLIC, *Taking a Closer Look at the School Library Resource Centre*, SLIC, 1999, www.slainte.org.uk/Slicpubs/schoolpis.pdf.

Smith, A., *Accelerated Learning in Practice: brain based methods of accelerating motivation and achievement*, Network Educational Press, 1998.

Smith, A., *Accelerated Learning in the Classroom*, Network Educational Press, 1996.

Southcombe, D., *Setting the Scene: local studies resources in the school library: SLA guideline*, SLA, 1999.

Special Educational Needs and Disability Act 2001, The Stationery Office Ltd, www.hmso.gov.uk/acts/acts2001/20010010.htm.

Streatfield, D. and Markless, S., *Invisible Learning? the contribution of school libraries to teaching and learning*, British Library,1994.

Tilke, A. (ed.), *Library Association Guidelines for Secondary School Libraries*, Library Association Publishing, 1998.

Tilke, A., *On-the-job Sourcebook for School Librarians*, Library Association Publishing, 1998.

Tilke, A., *Managing Your School Library: a practical handbook*, Facet Publishing, 2002.

Tilke, A., *Taking Note: supporting music through the secondary school LRC: SLA guideline*, SLA, 2003.

Valentine, P. and Nelson, B., *Sneaky Teaching: the role of the school librarian*, British Library, 1988.

Van Riel, R., Getting past G, *Library & Information Update*, August 2002, 38–9.

Watson, L., Coffee, computers and cooperative learning, *Multi-media and Information Technology*, **29** (1) (February), 2003, 32–3.

Willars, G. and Parsons, B., *How to Monitor and Evaluate the School Library*, Leicestershire Library Services, 1997.

Williams, D., Wavell, C. and Coles, L., *Impact of School Library Services on Achievement and Learning: critical literature review*, The Robert Gordon University, 2001, www.resource.gov.uk/documents/impactsl.pdf.

Wynkworth, L. and Dubber, G., *Policy Making and Development Planning for the Secondary School LRC: SLA guideline*, SLA, 2003.

Appendix 1
Library policy template

Keep the policy short and simple, with bullet points wherever possible, and a couple of inspirational quotes that will remind everyone of the purpose of the school library.

School name
Date of policy (or latest revision)
1 The aims of the school library *Include here statements about the overall vision and what the service is setting out to achieve. Ensure that these aims link closely to the school's overall aims and vision. Ensure too that there is a key statement about who the library aims to serve.*
2 The key objectives for the school library *These could be medium-term aims or the main areas of service and focus for the school library (e.g. supporting the curriculum, providing for the wider curriculum, supporting individual students' skills, liaising with and working through teaching colleagues).* *They need to be developmental (e.g. to improve or increase rather than just to maintain), and measurable. They are the performance criteria against which progress will be measured.*
3 School library management and communication *Include here:* • *the management and staffing of the school library* • *networks and processes for consultation with users (staff and students)* • *links to other school committees and services* • *links to other school policies and the development plan.*
4 Access issues *Include here details about day-to-day access for students and teachers (opening hours, etc.). Specify the access for class groups. Also, outline the agreed induction programmes that are in place for the various year groups. Identify how the library is staffed at different times – what can students and staff expect? Outline the basic principles for, and the details of, the signing and guiding.*

(Continued overleaf)

5 Library use

This is the place to clarify any issues of policy regarding use of the library – the rules and regulations – but try to have only a few of these. Include a basic outline of use by staff. Identify any special conditions for using IT and other materials.

Identify any challenges and their solutions (e.g. equal access to IT for boys and girls; providing adequate support for students with special needs).

Outline the basic issues of marketing as it affects the library:

- *consulting with users and identifying needs*
- *clarifying details of the services that will meet these needs*
- *promoting the services to potential users*
- *reviewing services by involving users.*

Clarify any special issues relating to specific school policies or aims (e.g. the link to students' independent learning; the whole school information skills curriculum).

6 Resources, accommodation and finance

Identify standards relating to resource provision in the school – the stock, the accommodation, the space and the equipment that are needed at a basic level. If possible, include benchmarks provided by information from other schools or supplied by the SLS, or from national publications. Include an outline of an annual budget bid, showing how it is developed and the main elements that the budget needs to cover.

7 Support and partnerships

List any support agencies and contacts used (such as the SLS, Connexions, or local libraries and museums or education centres). Identify the membership of professional associations as appropriate.

8 Monitoring and evaluation

List any performance measures and performance indicators you use on a regular basis. Identify the ways in which the library seeks feedback from users (staff and students), and the ways in which the quality of the service is tested and measured. Keep a list of the key achievements over the past three years, and a list of the main developments towards which the library is aiming. The short-term and medium-term ones will feature in the library development plan, but the longer-term aims can at least be discussed when the policy is reviewed annually. Identify the ways in which the library policy will itself be reviewed on a regular annual basis.

Name

Signature

Post

Date of next review

Appendix 2
Development plan template

Development plan targets should be tied to the targets for the whole school and to the aims and objectives in the library policy. They need to indicate the human and financial resources required and to be measurable.

Contributing area: Library   **Year:** 2004

Targets	Strategy	Human resources	Financial resources	Professional development	Success criteria	Evaluation	Date for completion
Improve post-16 achievement through developing information-literacy skills	• Purchase network licence of mind-mapping software	Librarian and head of IT to train students	£900 from central funds for whole-school resource	Hold staff INSETs by department to train teachers	Software purchased, staff and students trained; teachers incorporating use in schemes of work; student outcomes improved	Librarian, post-16 manager, heads of departments	June 2004
	• Develop post-16 induction to include evaluation of internet sources.	Development time for librarian	£150 for course Photocopying	Librarian to attend course re effective use of the internet Discuss with departments strategies to take the evaluation of sources into the curriculum	Students critical of information they find; able to apply criteria	Librarian, post-16 manager, heads of departments	December 2004
Improve ICT provision	• Negotiate with IT for upgraded access in library	Librarian, systems manager	Convert network connection from a hub to a switch @ £500 Increase individual machines' memory from 256 Mb to 512 Mb @ £50 each		Memory sticks and switch installed; student access time reduced	Librarian	October 2004
Resource new courses in GCSE Drama and AVCE Tourism	• Discuss with staff the schemes of work and the resources required • Weed collection of out-of-date material • Purchase relevant resources	Librarian, relevant teaching staff	50 volumes per course @ £13 = £1300. Electronic resources at £400 (to be negotiated as whole-school spend or shared with departments)		Items purchased; students and staff familiar with them and making use of them	Librarian, teaching staff, students	December 2004

Appendix 3
Sample job description for a secondary school librarian

Post title

School Librarian / Information and Learning Resources Manager

Prime objectives of the post

1. To manage a learning resource centre that incorporates print, online and e-learning resources and contributes to the learning targets of the school, growing in line with educational initiatives.
2. To participate in school-wide development through the regular cycle of meetings with senior staff.
3. To generate and implement the library development plan and to manage the library budget.
4. To act as a co-educator by teaching staff and students the skills of information literacy within curricular contexts, particularly collaborating in the design and delivery of resource-based learning experiences.
5. To act as an information navigator by selecting appropriate resources in all formats and bridging the gaps between students and teachers and online/electronic information, the curriculum and subject teaching.
6. To develop the library's contribution to literacy programmes and to inspire and enthuse students to read widely.
7. To maintain and develop a working knowledge of educational initiatives, information and communications technologies and developments in school librarianship.

Responsible for:
Staff

1. Supervise and appraise library assistants.
2. Supervise any trainees on placement for the NVQ qualification in Information and Library Services.
3. Supervise and train student library assistants.

Statutory, within the context of the department

1. Health and safety
2. Data protection
3. Conformity to copyright.

Responsible to:

Deputy Head Teacher with responsibility for the curriculum.

Person Specification

Experience

At least two years working in a school or college library.

Qualifications

- Chartered member of CILIP: the Chartered Institute of Library and Information Professionals
- Degree or postgraduate qualification in librarianship or information management.

Knowledge, skills, abilities

At interview the candidate needs to be able to demonstrate experience in the following areas:

- secondary education with an awareness of current issues and trends
- reading interests of secondary students and reader-development initiatives
- information-literacy teaching
- development planning, monitoring and evaluation
- budget management
- health and safety issues
- library management systems
- advocacy and vision
- ICT competence to ECDL level or equivalent
- time management
- behaviour management
- materials selection in all formats.

Personal and physical qualities

- likes teenagers
- good interpersonal skills and confident communicator
- experienced team worker
- enthusiastic, self-motivated and flexible
- able to work at shelves from floor level to 2 m in height, to pack and unpack boxes of books, etc.

This section will also include the employer's standard statement regarding equal opportunities and the candidate's availability to work the required hours and to participate in school events.

Appendix 4
Sample template for budget planning

Example for a school of 1000 students with a current library stock of 10,000 items.

(All figures are illustrative only, and are estimated.)

Current library stock 10,000 vols		
Budget needs for coming year:		£
New curriculum courses • GCSE Drama • AVCE – Tourism	needs 50 vols @ £13 needs 50 vols @ £13	650 650
10% replacement stock per year	1000 @ £12 per vol. average – paperbacks and hardbacks	12,000
SLS subscription	Use of 1000 exchangeable vols plus range of services	500
On-line subscriptions	Using e-learning credits	400
Newspapers and magazines • Daily newspaper • 25 journals	38 weeks only Annual subscriptions	100 2500
Total for learning resources	**(£16.80 per student)**	**16,800**
Stationery and display materials		500
Photocopy/printer paper		800
Equipment: new furniture		850
Author visit and reader-development activity	(To be matched by sponsorship)	150
Total for equipment and stationery		**2,300**
Total required for year	**(£19.10 per student)**	**19,100**

Appendix 5

Risk assessment form

Risk assessment for	Assessment undertaken on	Assessment review	Assessment undertaken by
Library	Date: 11/10/03	Date: 11/10/04	Librarian
List of significant hazards	**List groups of people who are at risk from the significant hazards you have identified and possible consequences**	**Action needed to prevent hazard**	**Action taken**
Loose carpet tiles	Students All College staff Visitors	See Site Manager to arrange fixing down	Tiles secured 11/10/03
Possible overloading of shelves	Same	Arrange inspection by Health and Safety officer	Inspection held; balanced load and width of base adequate for shelves to be deemed safe 10/12/03
Health and safety risk to staff from carrying too many books at once	Library staff	Purchase of additional book trolley to move books being re-shelved	Trolley purchased, staff instructed in proper loading. Staff also instructed to use it whenever moving more than six books at a time 15/11/03
Behaviour management in library a problem and possible risk at peak times of use	Students Library staff	Discussion with Health and Safety officer; conduct usage survey at peak times over a two week period; meeting with senior management to present findings and seek solutions	Teaching staff assigned to permanent rota in the library at peak times 12/01/03

Nature of risk assessment: Library

Signed: _____   _____

      Health and Safety officer   Date

Appendix 6

E-learning and virtual learning environments

E-learning

E-learning is a method of learning that focuses on accessing content through an online computer connection, submitting assignments or other work electronically, and receiving remote support from teachers or tutors through telephone or e-mail contact.

E-learning is developing fast in the business world, for adult learning (e.g. LearnDirect) and in further and higher education. It also has important implications for secondary schools. There are potential advantages for schools in rural environments and at post-16 where student numbers can limit the range of courses that can be offered at any one institution. However, successful e-learning requires carefully developed content, effective online links (preferably over a broadband network) and adequate tutor support. Occasional face to face (perhaps through video conferencing) student–tutor contact is essential to support effective teaching and learning.

Virtual learning environments

A virtual learning environment (VLE) is an online framework for managing learning. It can provide content, support material, communications, online exercises, student assessments and an evaluation of progress and achievements across a group of learners. The VLE provides an accessible bank of information and resources to support student learning, as well as the full range of exercises and work assignments that are needed for students to progress their learning. It can offer:

- communication between student and teacher,
- the option of web-based discussion lists
- automated assessment of student work
- a management overview of the learning that is taking place for teachers with administrative rights to the system.

VLEs are being used in further and higher education to provide support to a range of courses and programmes. Tutors can deposit lecture notes and assignment details, and can build weblinks to internal and external resources for further reading. Students can contribute to discussion lists about their subjects, and ask questions of their tutors.

In secondary schools, VLEs are most often used to complement traditional methods of teaching and learning. Some schools have used them to underpin basic literacy and numeracy skills, using online assessment to identify students in need of additional support at an early stage. This is where the great potential of the VLE to provide lesson delivery, curriculum content, student tracking and peer-to-peer or student-to-tutor interaction can produce cost effective diagnosis and can contribute to the improvement of students' skills. The structured online framework of a VLE can provide:

- lesson-authoring and question-design tools for use by teachers/tutors
- testing and assessment tools and progress records for individual students
- attractive templates and graphics to enhance the design of teaching resources
- lesson delivery through interactive whiteboards, computer suites and individual PCs
- lessons delivered remotely, e.g. in the school or public library, and at home
- quality assured lessons already prepared for supply teachers
- improved organization through electronic diaries and personal storage areas
- access for the whole-school community – staff, students, parents and governors
- security controlled by passwords and protocols set by the VLE administrator (usually the school's network manager).

At this point in time, no VLE standards exist. It is an emergent market in which we can expect rapid change. The software solutions currently available will evolve and develop (for example, pilot projects taking place at the time of writing in South Yorkshire and Bradford are involved in assessing software quality and management issues relating to some of these products).

Managed learning environments

There is sometimes confusion between VLEs and managed learning environments (MLEs). Whereas VLEs have been defined as 'environments that encompass online interactions of various kinds that take place between learners and tutors ... including online learning, the term MLE is more inclusive. An MLE includes 'the whole range of systems and processes ... that contribute directly or indirectly to learning and the management of that learning'.[1] MLEs can include all the functions of a VLE as well as all the administrative systems and networks that support a school or college. They will include the networking, intranet (i.e. internal web-based system), extranet (selective external web-based system, e.g. accessible for parents and governors), and internet access for the institution, presented in one integrated package and easily accessible through the desktops of the institution's PCs.

The implications for the school library

It is the library's role to support the whole curriculum. The library catalogue is key to making all resources more accessible over the school intranet and through a VLE or MLE. This will also enable the future development of online library services (e.g. reservations, enquiries) and effective links to further resources (e.g. external or cached websites, online subscription resources, or information held in the local community). Where VLEs are being used, it will be important to ensure appropriate links to library information and resources. This includes providing added value information to VLE managers to ensure appropriate library expertise and learning resources are used to support the managed learning.

Because of their cross-curricular role and their understanding of issues surrounding independent learning and resource management, school librarians are in a key position to influence developments in their own institutions. School librarians need to be aware of and involved in VLE and MLE planning and development in their schools. Key people to talk to are the headteacher, the senior teacher in charge of curriculum, the school's network manager, and the senior teacher in charge of ICT. The key message is that a VLE or MLE needs to encompass the school library to assist students in accessing the wider resources that will help them with their learning. This enables the school to make the most effective use of the significant investment made in its online environment.

Reference

1 *JISC Briefing Paper no. 1*, www.jisc.ac.uk/index.cfm?name=mle_briefings_1.

Appendix 7

Facilities management checklist

Area	In place	Planned/date	Comment
Shelving			
To meet requirements for accessibility:			
• Maximum height 1500 mm (walls)			
• Maximum height 1200 mm (island units)			
• Sufficient space between bays to accommodate wheelchairs			
• Fully adjustable shelving throughout the library			
• Display shelves included (preferably one per bay)			
• Shelf depth adequate for stock (min. 200 mm for fiction; 250 mm for non-fiction)			
• Standard sized bays throughout, to allow for easy interchanging of shelves			
• Clear sight lines			
• Flexibility: — Ability to add units and equipment (display panels and flat walling) — Mobile units (castors)			
• Shelving units to suit all resource types: — CDs, DVDs — Videos — Audio cassettes — Newspapers, magazines — Pamphlets, posters — Paperbacks			
Signing and guiding			
• Exterior notices and displays about the library			
• Map of library near entrance			
• Large hanging signs indicating different zones			
• Large bay headings to identify different stock areas			
• Clear shelf guides			
• Adjustable seats at computers, positioned to enable supervision			
• Some adjustable computer desks and tables, suitable for wheelchair users			

(*Continued overleaf*)

102 The CILIP Guidelines for Secondary School Libraries

Area	In place	Planned/Date	Comment
Equipment			
• Self-issue and dedicated enquiry terminals			
• Dedicated library staff terminals for the library management system			
• Sufficient workstations with school network and internet connections to accommodate at least one-half of a class at any one time			
• Photocopier			
• Printers and scanners			
• Telephone and fax machines			
• PCs connected to the internet			
• Standalone PCs for specialist curriculum software not generally available on the network			
• Multimedia projector, interactive whiteboard, etc.			
Security			
• Lockers/coat racks outside the library or just inside the entrance			
• Security mirrors			
• Use of CCTV			
• Installation of electronic security system (proves to be cost effective through loss reduction in most schools in 2–3 years, evidenced by annual stocktakes)			
• ICT hardware secured			
• Audio/visual equipment in locked storage when not in use			
Health and Safety (see Risk Assessment template in Appendix 5)			
Fire			
• Exit routes uncluttered			
• Sufficient fire extinguishers — Regularly tested — Staff trained in use			
• Smoke alarms installed and tested			
• Fire drill procedure notice on display			
• Library inductions to include evacuation instructions			

(Continued on facing page)

Appendix 7 Facilities management checklist

Area	In place	Planned/Date	Comment
Shelving			
• Secured into position			
• Not overloaded or top-heavy			
• Castors on mobile units always locked			
• No exposed edges on display shelves			
• Trolleys loaded evenly			
• All stock within easy reach			
Furniture			
• All of fire resistant/non-toxic material			
• Appropriate height or adjustable (users with disabilities catered for)			
• Trolleys designed for stability and used with care			
• Carpets and flooring securely fixed			
Technology and equipment			
• No trailing cables or exposed/damaged wiring			
• All electrical equipment checked annually			
Insurance			
• Library contents insured to replacement cost			
• Library staff insured appropriately for supervision of student numbers			

Appendix 8
Research grid

This is an extremely flexible tool, which can be used at a multitude of levels for a variety of tasks. The idea is to give students a topic, or a big question, then help them to develop their own smaller questions to provide a focus for their research. Their sources are noted down the side and become a ready bibliographic reference. Using A3 paper, either printed or simply folded in half four times, the squares on the grid become the frame for note taking.

Topic What was life in England like during World War II?	Question 1 What kinds of jobs did women do?	Question 2 What foods were rationed and why?	Question 3 How did family life change?
Source 1			
Source 2			
Source 3			
Source 4			

Appendix 9
Mind mapping

This map was done with Inspiration (www.inspiration.com). The big question was posed to a group of students who then broke it down into subsidiary questions, starting from a factual base of 'What is cloning?' to the complex issue of who would fund such activity and what their motives might be. This type of visual tool can be used by a group to discuss and develop issues, projecting onto a whiteboard and altering the map as ideas emerge, or it can be used by individuals to develop ideas, organize thinking, take notes and develop essay plans.

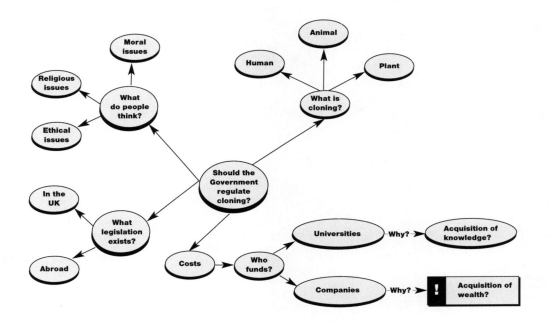

Index

access, learning resources 34–5
advocacy 64–5
    see also marketing
AIDA see *A*wareness, *I*nterest, *D*esire, *A*ction
Area Guidelines for Schools, facilities
        management 27–8
*A*wareness, *I*nterest, *D*esire, *A*ction (AIDA),
        promotion management 60–1

behaviour management 16–17
bibliography 85–9
book trade, partnerships 82
brain-based reading, reader development 50
budgets
    Empowerment Pack for School Libraries
        35–6
    learning resources 35–6
    management 14–15
    materials fund 19–20
    planning 96
    template 96
    see also financial planning

capital projects, financial planning 14
careers services, partnerships 82
CILIP, vision 1–5
colour, facilities management 25–6
committees, library, policy/development
        planning 10
Connexions, partnerships 82
consultation, evaluation 72
continuous professional development (CPD)
        15–16
costing management, marketing 60
CPD *see* continuous professional
        development
culture, reading 51–3
curricula
    information literacy 39–45
    reading 48–50

demand forecasting/management, marketing
        59–60
development
    information literacy 43–4
    reader 47–54

development planning
    financial planning 13
    school libraries 7–10
    template 93
    see also management
display, facilities management 29
drinking and eating, facilities management 25

e-learning, ICT 20, 98
eating and drinking, facilities management 25
educational initiatives, financial planning 13
Empowerment Pack for School Libraries, resources
    35–6
endorsement, policy/development planning 10
environment and function, facilities management
    23–30
evaluation 67–76
    approaches 72–5
    benefits 76
    consultation 72
    external 74–5
    impacts 71–2
    inputs 69–70
    managing 68–9
    outcomes 71–2
    outputs 70–1
    peer review 74
    reader development 49
    recommendations 67
    results 75–6
    self-evaluation 49, 72–4
external evaluation 74–5

facilitating learning 2–4
facilities management 23–30
    checklist 101–3
    function and environment 23–30
    recommendations 23
feeder schools, partnerships 81
financial planning 13–15
    see also budgets
function and environment, facilities management
    23–30
further learning institutions, partnerships 81–2
further reading 85–9
future planning, financial planning 14

governors, promotion to 62
guidelines, financial planning 13

hardware, ICT 20
heating, facilities management 25
higher learning institutions, partnerships 81–2

historical spend, financial planning 14
human resources, management 15–16, 94–5

ICT see information and communication technology
impacts, evaluation 71–2
information and communication technology (ICT)
    e-learning 20, 98
    hardware 20
    information literacy 20, 41–2
    management 17–20
    materials fund 19–20
    MLEs 18–19, 99–100
    reader development 50–1
    staff 20
    stock 19
    VLEs 18–19, 33, 98–100
information literacy 37–45
    curricula 39–45
    educational imperative 39–42
    ICT 20, 41–2
    implementing 42–3
    resources 44
    skills 37–45
    successful development 43–4
inputs, evaluation 69–70
INSET, marketing 63

job description, librarians 94–5

learning
    defined 1
    e-learning 20, 98
    environment and function 23–30
    facilitating 2–4
    facilities management 23–30
    motivating 3
    opportunities 2
    supporting 2–4
learning resources 31–6
    access 34–5
    budgets 35–6
    context 31–2
    location 32
    needs assessment 32–3
    organization 34–5
    policies 33–4
    selection 33–4
leisure reading 3
librarians
    advocacy 64–5
    job description 94–5
    management responsibilities (categories) 12
    as mediators 2–4

roles 2-4, 42-3, 64-5
as teachers 3
library policy template 91-2
lighting, facilities management 24
literacy, information *see* information literacy
location and use, facilities management 26-7
location, learning resources 32

managed learning environments (MLEs) 18-19, 99-100
management
  behaviour 16-17
  budgets 14-15
  financial planning 13-15
  human resources 15-16, 94-5
  ICT 17-20
  learning resources 31-6
  promotion 60-4
  recommendations 12
  school libraries 11-21
  structure 11-12
  VLEs 18-19
  see also development planning
management responsibilities (categories), librarians 12
marketing 55-66
  AIDA 60-1
  costing management 60
  defined 55
  demand forecasting/management 59-60
  INSET 63
  marketing mix 56-7
  planning 57-64
  promotion management 60-4
  recommendations 55
  resource management 60
  SWOT analysis 57, 58
materials fund, ICT 19-20
mind mapping 105
MLEs *see* managed learning environments
monitoring, evaluation 68
motivating learning 3
movement, facilities management 25

needs analysis, marketing planning 57-9
needs assessment, learning resources 32-3
neighbouring schools 82
A New Specialist System: transforming secondary education 2
noise, facilities management 24-5

objectives, evaluation 69
Ofsted (Office for Standards in Education) 67, 74

opportunities, learning 2
organization, learning resources 34-5
outcomes, evaluation 71-2
outputs, evaluation 70-1

parent teacher associations (PTAs) 80-1
parents
  partnerships 80-1
  promotion to 63-4
partnerships 4, 77-83
  book trade 82
  careers services 82
  Connexions 82
  feeder schools 81
  further learning institutions 81-2
  higher learning institutions 81-2
  parents 80-1
  public libraries 82
  recommendations 77
  successful 82-3
  youth services 82
PAT *see* Professional Association of Teachers
peer review, evaluation 74
performance indicators, evaluation 68-9
performance measures, evaluation 68
planning
  budgets 96
  financial 13-15
  marketing 57-64
  school libraries 7-10
  stakeholder involvement 9-10
policies
  learning resources 33-4
  library policy template 91-2
  school 11-12
  school libraries 7-10
  stakeholder involvement 9-10
  templates 91-3
primary schools 4
Professional Association of Teachers (PAT), behaviour management 16-17
progress reporting, evaluation 69
promotion 55-66
  AIDA 60-1
  management 60-4
  methods 61-4
  see also marketing
PTAs *see* parent teacher associations
public libraries, partnerships 82

reader development 47-54
  ICT 50-1
  websites 53

reading culture 51–3
reading curriculum, school libraries 48–50
recommendations
    evaluation 67
    facilities management 23
    information literacy 37
    learning resources 31, 36
    management 12, 17
    marketing 55
    partnerships 77
    reader development 47
research grid 104
resource management, marketing 60
resources
    advocacy 65
    facilities management 23–30
    information literacy 44
    see also learning resources
risk assessment form 97
roles 1–5, 8, 42–3, 64–5

school libraries
    development planning 7–10
    management 11–21
    policy 7–10
    reading curriculum 48–50
    roles 1–5, 8, 43
    and wider learning community 4
School Library Manifesto 1, 31
schools library services (SLSs) 4
    best use of 79–80
    partnerships 77–80
    services 78–9
self-evaluation 72–4
    reader development 49
senior management, promotion to 62
signage, facilities management 28–9
skills, information literacy 37–45
SLSs *see* schools library services

space requirements, facilities management 27–8
staff, ICT 20
stakeholder involvement
    planning 9–10
    policy 9–10
standards
    financial planning 13
    literacy 41
Start with the Child 23, 37
stock, ICT 19
students, promotion to 61–2
Survey of Secondary School Libraries 15
SWOT analysis, marketing 57, 58

targets, evaluation 69
teaching staff, promotion to 62–3
templates
    budgets 96
    development planning 93
    library policy 91–2
    policies 91–3
training, CPD 15–16

user consultation, policy/development planning 10

virtual learning environments (VLEs) 98–100
    learning resources 33
    management 18–19
vision, CILIP's 1–5
VLEs *see* virtual learning environments

websites, reader development 53
wider learning community
    promotion to 63–4
    school libraries and 4
work area, facilities management 24

youth services, partnerships 82